BUILDING
STRONG
SCHOOL CULTURES

Leadership for Learning

Series Editors
Willis D. Hawley and E. Joseph Schneider

Please call our toll-free number (800-818-7243)
or visit our Web site (www.corwinpress.com)
to order individual titles or the entire series.

BUILDING STRONG SCHOOL CULTURES

A GUIDE TO LEADING CHANGE

SHARON D. KRUSE
KAREN SEASHORE LOUIS

A Joint Publication

For information:

Corwin Press
A SAGE Publications Company
2455 Teller Road
Thousand Oaks, California 91320
www.corwinpress.com

SAGE Ltd.
1 Oliver's Yard
55 City Road
London EC1Y 1SP
United Kingdom

SAGE India Pvt. Ltd.
B 1/I 1 Mohan Cooperative
    Industrial Area
Mathura Road, New Delhi
India 110 044

SAGE Asia-Pacific Pte. Ltd.
33 Pekin Street #02-01
Far East Square
Singapore 048763

Printed in the United States of America.

Library of Congress Cataloging-in-Publication Data

Kruse, Sharon D.
Building strong school cultures : a guide to leading change/Sharon D. Kruse, Karen Seashore Louis; Joint publication with the American Association of School Administrators (AASA).
    p. cm. — (Leadership for learning series)
Includes bibliographical references and index.
ISBN 978-1-4129-5181-4 (cloth)
ISBN 978-1-4129-5182-1 (pbk.)
    1. School environment—United States. 2. Community and school—United States. 3. School improvement programs—United States. 4. Educational change—United States. I. Louis, Karen Seashore. II. Title. III. Series.

LC203.K78 2009
370.190973—dc22   2008019166

This book is printed on acid-free paper.

08   09   10   11   12   10   9   8   7   6   5   4   3   2   1

Acquisitions Editor:	Arnis Burvikovs
Associate Editor:	Desirée A. Bartlett
Editorial Assistant:	Irina Dragut
Production Editor:	Jane Haenel
Copy Editor:	Trey Thoelcke
Typesetter:	C&M Digitals (P) Ltd.
Proofreader:	Anne Rogers
Indexer:	Karen McKenzie
Cover Designer:	Michael Dubowe

Contents

Series Foreword

This book by Sharon D. Kruse and Karen Seashore Louis is one of a series edited as part of the Leadership for Learning initiative of the American Association of School Administrators (AASA). Its primary purpose is to provide school leaders with support in strategic allocation of limited resources to maximize student performance and foster continuous school improvement.

School leaders who pick up *Building Strong School Cultures: A Guide to Leading Change* will wish they had read it first before they had digested the many books that promised to develop them into "heroic" school leaders.

The basic premise of this book is that the principal's job is more than any one person can be expected to do well. The recent explosion of expectations and tasks loaded on school leaders, the authors argue, has made the job next to impossible. It's even too much for a leadership team.

The authors, both well steeped in the leadership literature from their years of research and writing, don't flinch when they talk about what it takes to lead a successful school. An effective school leader is expected to:

- provide and sell a vision;
- provide encouragement and recognition;
- obtain resources;
- adapt standard operating procedures;
- monitor the improvement effort; and
- handle disturbances.

Some of these functions are about promoting change; some clearly are about maintenance (e.g., providing encouragement and handling disturbances). But one thing is for sure, ensuring stability while promoting continuous improvement is very difficult.

Principals today have to concern themselves with the community as well as with school professionals. That interaction with parents and community service agencies cannot be just public relations anymore either. The authors argue, "Deep-seated changes in the culture of schools are unlikely to occur without action to create more fundamental bonds with the community." But even that isn't sufficient. Increasingly, the principals are expected to make their schools full-service providers of health and social services; schools are being asked to partner with the business community and other agencies to offer programs from on-site preschools to networks of service learning and internship opportunities.

School leaders once had the luxury of focusing on students in the classroom. Now, the authors say, the school leaders' focus is much broader, one that emphasizes the connections of the school with the wider world of foundations, business groups, social service providers, and government agencies.

Having bonded with their reader about the challenges of the job, Sharon D. Kruse and Karen Seashore Louis slip easily into a discussion about how to tackle it successfully.

The authors believe school leaders need to move beyond the current pressure to focus on curriculum and instruction. Rather, school leaders ought to concentrate on integrating the fragmented subcultures that exist in every school. They don't have to become anthropologists. But principals need to understand: "It is the influence of peers, parents, colleagues, and community that creates a fidgeting, rebellious student or a burned-out and cynical teacher. Nothing inherent in a classroom creates these realities, nor can classroom teaching alone cause them to disappear."

The book introduces a new approach for changing the cultural conditions of a school that they say will affect teaching and learning. The authors call it "intensification of leadership."

Simply put, intensification of leadership is a way to increase the number of people engaged in leadership roles and the scope of the school's work as it relates to student outcomes. The term, the authors say, "assumes that there is a deliberately broadened meaningful involvement—through job redesign and through the permanent redistribution of the work. . . . The implication is that there is no longer a single leader, or even a small leadership team. Intensified leadership suggests that leadership roles must meaningfully and purposefully be inhabited by the many."

Kruse and Louis say their leadership model extends beyond the school too. "Intensified leadership opens the boundaries of leadership to include, in ongoing and permanent ways, a wide variety of members of the school and the surrounding community in new decision-making roles, and it asks them to become involved in generating new kinds of decisions and practices rather than simply carrying out existing functions. Jobs and roles are enlarged, and the range and type of decisions that can be made at all levels and by a variety of parties is increased."

To assist the school leader, the authors introduce them to three conditions for constructing school cultures captured by the acronym PCOLT: professional community, organizational learning, and trust.

The concept of professional community grows out of earlier work the two authors have done. They argue that "strong school cultures are based on shared norms and values, reflective dialogue, public practice, and collaboration."

Organizational learning is the concept that collective engagement with new ideas will generate enhanced classroom practices and deeper understanding of how organizational improvement occurs.

Trust is the glue. "In schools, trust is considered to be the result of several dispositions working in concert. Among these are integrity (or honesty and openness), concern (also called benevolence or personal regard for others), competence, and reliability (or consistency)," maintain the authors.

The book is chock full of case studies and practical advice. It wraps up with an admonishment not to go for the school improvement "quick fix" (the authors acknowledge, as administrators themselves, how seductive it can be). The pressure to raise test scores can be unbearable. However, the authors buy into the old adage: "If it seems too good to be true, it is." Effective, lasting change in the school's culture takes time. But it is the only way to ensure ongoing, improved student learning.

Kruse and Louis explore with their readers some of the "false hopes" leaders embrace in their eagerness to improve their schools' cultures. They worry that "embracing quick fixes fosters a belief in leaders that they are doing the best they can for the students in their schools." The authors prefer to have school leaders acknowledge that nurturing pipe dreams just weakens their ability to engage in real change.

Willis D. Hawley
E. Joseph Schneider

Acknowledgments

This book is the product of nearly twenty years of collaboration between the authors. It is also the product of our individual work over a combined fifty years of working in and studying schools. As such, it is not the result of a single project but emerges from our ongoing reflections on intersections in our work over time. When we saw each other, we'd mention an interesting finding or an emerging trend in our most recent data set. The ensuing discussions helped us to understand our own work better, and almost always ended with a promise to collaborate on a more formal presentation. In many ways, this book is the result of those discussions, as well as our individual projects and interests. It is also the product of our extended preoccupation with making schools better places for adults and children. We begin by acknowledging each other and the richness of our personal and professional partnership.

A Faculty Improvement Leave awarded by the University of Akron for the fall 2007 semester also supported the writing of this book. The support of the Department of Educational Foundations and Leadership and the College of Education in the application of leave materials is greatly appreciated. Jane Beese, who carefully read the early chapters of the text and offered a careful yet encouraging critique, provided further support. Karen's work was facilitated by a sabbatical leave from the University of Minnesota, but is also enriched by her work with colleagues and students, both in the United States and other countries, whose thinking continues to shape her thinking about leadership and organizational culture. They are too numerous to mention individually, but they know who they are.

Without Dan Bratton's editorial assistance, our words would be less precise and our sentences longer; we appreciate his ability to cut our ideas down to size. Taylor Kruse took Sharon's author photo and she appreciates his skill and willingness to do so.

At Corwin Press, we would like to thank Irina Dragut and Arnis Burvikovs, who stewarded the manuscript through its many drafts. As series editors, Willis Hawley and Joe Schneider provided us early and important feedback; we thank them for their assistance.

Finally, without the many classrooms and schools we have been allowed to visit, this book could not be possible. We thank the teachers, principals, parents, and district leadership who provided us access to classrooms and sat for our interviews and questions. Throughout this book we have drawn from those experiences, using their words and examples. As promised to them, all of our examples carry pseudonyms.

PUBLISHER'S ACKNOWLEGMENTS

Corwin Press gratefully acknowledges the contributions of the following individuals:

Mary K. Culver
Assistant Clinical Professor
Northern Arizona University
Flagstaff, AZ

Lyman Goding
Visiting Lecturer
Bridgewater State College
Bridgewater, MA, and
Retired Principal
Community Intermediate School
Plymouth, MA

Teresa Cunningham
Principal
Laurel Elementary School
Laurel Bloomery, TN

James L. Pate
Associate Professor
Valdosta State University
Valdosta, GA

About the Authors

Sharon D. Kruse is a professor in the Department of Educational Foundations and Leadership at the University of Akron. Over the past decade she has studied school leadership and successful school improvement practices. She previously worked with Karen Seashore Louis coauthoring *Professionalism and Community: Perspectives on Reforming Urban Schools* from Corwin Press (1995), and with Bob Johnson, Jr., coauthoring *Decision Making for Educational Leaders: Under-Examined Dimensions and Issues*.

Karen Seashore Louis is Rodney S. Wallace Professor for the Advancement of Teaching and Learning at the University of Minnesota. For the past thirty-five years, her research has focused on school improvement and reform, leadership in school settings, and knowledge-use in education. Her most recent books are *Organizing for School Change* (2006), *Aligning Student Support With Achievement Goals: The Secondary School Principal's Guide* (with Molly Gordon, 2006), and *Professional Learning Communities: Divergence, Depth and Dilemmas* (with Louise Stoll, 2007). A two-time Davis Award winner for the best article in the *Educational Administration Quarterly*, Louis has also served on the executive board for the University Council for Educational Administration and as vice president of the American Educational Research Association.

To:
All of the educators who have participated in our research over the years, without whose stories and experiences this book would not have been written.

And to:
Dan Bratton from Karen—whose careful review of sections of this book improved my prose.

Stan and Ruth Youth from Sharon—whose guidance over the years has proved invaluable.

1

Changing School Culture

An Introduction and Overview

The message of this book for principals is research based and practical. We argue that school leaders must move beyond the current pressure to place exclusive priority on curriculum and instruction and, instead, focus on integrating and focusing the fragmented subcultures that exist in any school. It is the influence of peers, parents, colleagues, and community that creates a fidgeting, rebellious student or a burned-out and cynical teacher. Nothing inherent in a classroom creates these realities, nor can classroom teaching alone cause them to disappear.

Intensification of leadership is our term to describe an approach to changing the cultural conditions that affect teaching and learning. We are not advocating the abandonment of instructional leadership; principals clearly need to understand and support what teachers do in classrooms in order to help create the conditions that allow them to be more effective. Intensification of leadership acknowledges the existing reality that there are already multiple leaders in any school, and offers a road map to integrate these influences into a more coherent and less contradictory message.

There is a fundamental problem, however: you cannot control your school's culture. Most of the people—teachers, students, and parents—who collectively determine what the school's culture is like have limited incentive to listen to you. Managing a school's culture is not dependent on

1

the *authority* that you have based on your position, but can only be affected by increasing your *influence* over behaviors, beliefs, relationships, and other complex dynamics present in the school that are often unpredictable.

Before we begin to examine schools that have made lasting cultural change, we offer a caveat. It is beyond the scope of this effort to assess the issues of changes in educational policy or public attitudes that provide the backdrop for principal's work but over which they have little influence. Nor do we deal with schools in crisis; those in which academic performance and teacher morale suggest a need for a dramatic "fresh start." The issues we address will be those facing the vast majority of "typical schools" and "typical school administrators."

There is a tradition in the school reform literature that treats elementary schools, middle schools, and high schools as if they are vastly different places. While this is true when the discussion focuses on specific curricular or instructional strategies, such as the efficacy of early reading programs or AP coursework, our research (and that of others) suggests that schools have much in common. Every principal faces similar challenges when faced with changing the "way we have always done things here." It doesn't matter if an elementary school adopts 4-block reading or a high school implements block scheduling, school leaders will face similar forms of resistance, skepticism, and challenge. The old adage that high schools teach subjects and elementary schools teach children is countered by the finding that grade and other teams exert influences in elementary schools that can be every bit as powerful as those of departments at the secondary level.

To illustrate our approach, throughout the book we will consider cases drawn from real schools and principals who have done things right—or were blindsided by unanticipated events and consequences of their own actions. The authors of this book are researchers who have collectively spent more than fifty years trying to understand the world of teachers, administrators, and students. To understand these worlds, and to seek solutions to problems of practice, we have grounded our approach in organizational and management theories that were not specifically written for education. We have also been in the classroom and have worked directly with many schools and educational professionals, so we have the capacity to pull what is relevant from this broader and more abstract base. We hope that a novice school leader will find our analysis and recommendations useful to guide beginning efforts to take a more active role in shaping school cultures. We also expect that expert, experienced school leaders will read this book and find it affirming as they see themselves in our vignettes and recommendations.

This chapter will introduce the key assumptions, concepts, and topics that serve as the basis for the remainder of the book. How we perceive the nature of school culture is central to developing an intensification of leadership to change that culture. Just as physicists sometimes conceptualize light as a wave and sometimes as a particle, we will describe school cultures as both stable and fluid. We will introduce the acronym PCOLT to describe three key conditions for creating constructive school cultures: *p*rofessional *c*ommunity, *o*rganizational *l*earning, and *t*rust. At the end of make the new structure their own (and perhaps integrate some of the expertise that existed in the departments), could the interdisciplinary teams have struggled to find a new way of working? If the district curriculum coordinator had encouraged teachers to take responsibility for designing a school program that provided students with an interdisciplinary and personalized experience, but allowed time for within-subject curriculum development, could the transition have been managed by the staff themselves? Would providing opportunities in which tacit assumptions and values were surfaced and explored have helped to provide a bridge between what was culturally valued in the old structure and a dream for the new one? Culture is too complex to follow a static blueprint for change. What seems stable may shift as the social equations the actors have taken for granted are altered. Culture always will be the creation of its participants in response to each other and outside stimuli. For a culture to remain adaptive and fluid, the participants must have a hand in creating the new structures that grow out of the old. We hope that our book will provide you with the understanding and tools needed to develop strategies for addressing similar issues in your school.

One function of culture is to provide meaning and self-esteem, but a positive school culture does this as it improves organizational performance. This requires the principal to balance several foci. If the stakeholders in a school cannot take ownership of a change process, then self-esteem will be preserved by some form of blame on "the idiots that did this to us"—thereby absolving themselves of responsibility.

Figure 1.1 suggests that leadership in schools must balance an emphasis on creating stability and change, and between tending to the internal functioning of the school and paying attention to relationships with stakeholders outside.

We know that the typical principal will look at this figure and groan that it's just too much. Research suggests that this sense of overload is based on the real explosion of expectations and tasks for school administrators (Cooley & Shen, 2003; DiPaola & Tschannen-Moran, 2003). We agree with the typical principal: the leadership job that we have observed in today's schools is ever larger and ever more complicated, and no one person or administrative team can do it all. But rather than dividing up the existing leadership pie among more people, we suggest that the size of the pie also needs to be increased to include new tasks that are just beginning to emerge.

An up-to-date principal will have been inundated with popular and professional literature that emphasizes the need to set priorities and focus on instructional leadership. This usually means challenging teachers to improve curriculum and instruction, spending more time in classrooms, and mining data to provide evidence of how well the school is achieving its student-learning goals. Also, they also have to spend their time working on goals that are more clearly connected with more general school

Figure 1.1   Organizational Culture and Leadership

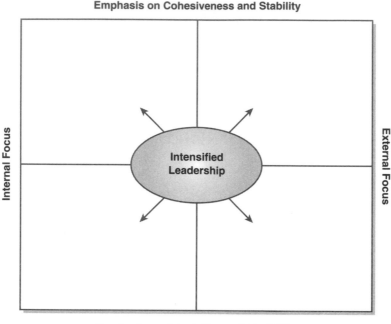

Emphasis on Cohesiveness and Stability

Internal Focus

External Focus

Intensified Leadership

Emphasis on Adaptation and Flexibility

climate, meeting state requirements, discipline, and organization (Whitaker & Turner, 2000). Studies of how effective principals operate when there is a high demand for change suggest that effective leaders enact six functions (Heller & Firestone, 1995):

1. Providing and selling a vision
2. Providing encouragement and recognition
3. Obtaining resources
4. Adapting standard operating procedures
5. Monitoring the improvement effort
6. Handling disturbances

A quick perusal of these functions suggest that some involve maintenance (for example, providing encouragement or handling disturbances), while others emphasize change (selling a vision and adapting school procedures).

Changing a school's culture to balance stability and change is not an easy task. A principal's ability to shift from the traditional internal priorities of curriculum, instruction, and maintaining a smooth and orderly environment is limited both by time constraints and the expectations of teachers. Current leadership literature suggests that there are solutions, such as establishing teacher professional learning communities and encouraging peer consultation and coaching, that can augment the principal's instructional role, but, without a great deal of attention to roadblocks and details, can easily be perceived as another temporary innovation that will pass (Hord & Sommers, 2008) or even what Andy Hargreaves calls "contrived collegiality" that is manipulated by administrators for their own purposes (Hargreaves & Dawe, 1990). Changing a school's internal culture demands that designated school leaders have real partners within the professional staff and that teachers want and exercise influence in areas outside the classroom.

In addition, resilient school improvement is more likely to occur if the principal focuses not just inside the school but also on redefining the relationship between *school professionals and their communities*. Evidence is increasing that effective school leaders are engaged with their local context and make student learning a task that can be supported by many. Principals occupy a singular position that permits them to act as boundary-spanners, creating solid links between the school (the primary site of formal student learning) and the community (the primary site of informal student learning). Creating bonds with other educators outside the school, through principal networks and more collaborative relationships with district office staff, can serve as a significant source of stimulation and reflective administrative practice. (We address these issues in Chapters 5, 6, and 7.)

Our perspective is broader than just increasing parental involvement or creating linkages with community service agencies, and we reject the dominant belief that interactions with the community should be driven by a public-relations focus that emphasizes successes, downplays failures, and limits transparency. Based on research, which we review in Chapter 7, we argue that the school's interpretive frame should shift away from looking at the community as a resource to support teachers and classrooms toward seeing it as a locus for student learning and development. In fact, we argue that deep-seated changes in the culture of schools are unlikely to occur without action to create more fundamental bonds with the community.

Creating community bonds and building trust with immediate stakeholders is no longer enough to ensure sustained support for a particular school and public education in general. Principals are increasingly expected to be entrepreneurial and to develop new alliances that can help schools meet their goals for student learning and development. Images of schools as full-service providers of health and social service care are plentiful in the school reform literature, and principals are looking for partners in business communities and other agencies to develop new programs ranging from on-site preschools to networks of service learning and internship opportunities. Never before have schools felt such pressure to support healthy youth development—at the same time that they are mandated to raise test scores. Most surveys do not measure the attention that principals give to this part of the job, and those that have indicate that principals still give this part of the job limited priority (Goldring & Hausman, 2001), but our informal observations suggest that this demand is increasing. This represents a dramatic shift in school culture because it changes the dynamic from one that is focused on students in classrooms to one that emphasizes the connections of the school with the wider world of foundations, business groups, social service providers, and government agencies.

INTRODUCING PCOLT—PROFESSIONAL COMMUNITY, ORGANIZATIONAL LEARNING, AND TRUST

School administrators are not anthropologists; they are concerned with school cultures as a means to positive outcomes. This book focuses on the cultural attributes of schools that create better opportunities for the students who attend. Thus, improving culture is not an end in itself, but the means by which school leaders can address the goals of student progress and achievement. Three features of school cultures that have been tied to student learning in multiple studies are:

1. *Professional community.* Professional community (PC) directs a spotlight on the relationships among adults within the school. By focusing on the structural and human resource conditions necessary for schools to become strongly connected around the goal of student learning, the framework suggests that strong school cultures are based on shared norms and values, reflective dialogue, public practice, and collaboration (Louis & Kruse, 1995). The essence of professional community is that all adults in a school are presented with the opportunity to work with others to grow and change—and that meaningful and sustained connections are necessary for that to occur. This occurs when teachers take collective responsibility for improving student learning. Collective responsibility, in which all members feel accountable for all students, is at the core of intensified leadership.

2. *Organizational learning.* The concept of organizational learning (OL) suggests that continuous improvement through collective engagement with new ideas will generate enhanced classroom practices and deeper understanding of how organizational improvement occurs. The idea is frequently coupled with that of professional community in programs that are designed to create more visible "professional learning communities" (Hord & Sommers, 2008; Stoll & Louis, 2007). However, not all group learning occurs in organized meetings, and we wish to emphasize the uncertainty of predicting which structures and experiences will produce the "aha moment" that helps to shift the culture from old to new values, beliefs, and practices. Seemingly random contacts with novel ideas, as well as structured efforts to examine data and plan new programs, may produce forward momentum. OL focuses on the ways in which new ideas are brought into the school organization, how they are considered and evaluated, and the ways in which school organizations retain and use the

knowledge generated from them. Organizational learning generally occurs when groups acknowledge small failures and consider alternatives, and this occurs more often when more people take responsibility for problem finding and problem solving (Levitt & March, 1988).

3. *Trust*. Trust is the glue that holds social networks and relationships together. In schools, trust is considered to be the result of several dispositions working in concert. Among these are integrity (or honesty and openness), concern (also called benevolence or personal regard for others), competence, and reliability (or consistency). Trust is also low in schools that feel beleaguered by public pronouncements that they are failing—not a message that is designed to create positive collaboration. Trust has been linked with organizational effectiveness in business settings; in schools, trust among teachers and between teachers and other groups is linked to higher student achievement (Tschannen-Moran, 2004). While principals cannot bear full responsibility for creating trusting cultures in their schools, their behavior sets a tone and a foundation for creating trusting relationships and professional community in other groups (Bryk & Schneider, 2002).

These ideas are increasingly familiar to school leaders and teachers, and many programs and staff development opportunities are designed to increase principal's ability to work with them. However the assumptions underlying PCOLT stand in stark contrast to the deeply embedded understanding of many school professionals about how schools should operate. Dan Lortie observed that teachers generally assume that they will work alone rather than with other adults, that the difference between their work and administrator's work constitutes a bright line that is seldom crossed (Lortie, 2002). Thus, there is a chasm between professional aspirations for dynamic and caring cultures and the reality encountered by many principals when they arrive at the schoolhouse door each morning.

Our research suggests that while many schools are working hard to develop school cultures characterized by professional community, organizational learning, and trust (which we refer to as PCOLT), there is a great deal of variation in the degree to which they have shifted their values away from older mental models. Cultivating these values can be a juggling act, and, as shown in the Corson example, a solid, positive culture can quickly erode when confronted with change. Our argument is that principals and other school leaders can guide their schools toward this goal and, once the school is moving in the right direction, help to sustain the momentum.

PCOLT is most powerful when the ideas that underscore each of the themes are viewed as strategic actions to build strong adaptive school cultures. Furthermore, our thinking positions PCOLT as an enduring approach to leadership behavior and temperament. Building a strong school culture is not something you do once, nor is PCOLT something you can claim to become—it is an orientation toward school leadership that sets the stage for achieving your goals for student success.

INTENSIFIED LEADERSHIP: AN INTRODUCTION

Employing PCOLT strategies requires a different kind of school leadership. We choose to call this form of leadership *intensified* because it increases the number of people engaged in leadership roles and the scope of the school's work as it relates to student outcomes. Other words been used to capture the changing nature of leadership in contemporary settings, ranging from shared leadership and site-based management, to servant and distributed leadership. Intensified leadership builds on the insights of these models.

Shared leadership and site-based management in most forms are limited to involving a variety of stakeholders in making decisions (Bauch & Goldring, 1998; Leithwood & Duke, 1998). Servant leadership, as a critical concept, emphasizes the role that formal leaders play in supporting the goals and work of others (Block, 1993). Mayrowetz and his colleagues distinguish between two ways of thinking about the distribution of leadership in a school. One *describes* how influence operates in schools—who has it and under what circumstances (Gronn, 2000; Spillane, Halverson, & Diamond, 2001), while the other *prescribes* sharing leadership as a means of reallocating the work of school improvement (Mayrowetz, Murphy, Louis, & Smylie, 2007).

In our view, the term *intensified leadership* combines both the descriptive and prescriptive perspective, and it unavoidably includes elements of shared and servant leadership. It assumes that *there is deliberately broadened meaningful involvement*—through job redesign and through the permanent redistribution of the work. It goes beyond saying that people will see their work as encompassing more tasks. By deepening their *collective responsibility* for finding and solving problems, selecting tasks and foci, people become more accountable for meshing the larger goals and vision of the school with the smaller tasks of daily leadership and management. Thus, it goes beyond simply giving the school's work to more people, and demands that all members of the school community become active decision makers. The implication is that there is no longer a single leader, or even a small leadership team. Intensified leadership suggests that leadership roles must meaningfully and purposefully be inhabited by the many. What this means in practice will become apparent as we present cases of leadership intensification through the remainder of the book.

Our notion of intensified leadership challenges the seductive image of the heroic leader. Traditionally, a hero or heroine "leads" by making critical decisions concerning organizational vision and goals, and sets a clear path for their attainment. Heroic leaders are portrayed as knowing the right thing to do and exactly when to do it. By making decisive choices and providing directions for others to accomplish these goals, heroic leaders motivate others to achieve success. This traditional representation of leadership positions the heroic leader as more intelligent, charismatic, and insightful than other members of the organization and holds the leader ultimately responsible for the success or failure of the organization. While the scholarly literature has trumpeted the demise of heroic leadership for several decades, the popular press continues to demand it and replacement terms such as "transformational leadership" (Bass, 1998) and "super-leadership" (Manz & Sims, 2001) do little to dispel the largely patriarchal image.

The problem with viewing leadership in this way is simple—it can't work in today's schools. The issues schools face are too complex, the pressures of day-to-day operations too complicated, and the stakes too high to suggest that an all-knowing leader—or even an all-knowing superleadership team—can succeed. Furthermore, this conception belies the truth of how school organizations work. From the office assistant who chooses to spend time with a parent new to the district, to the classroom teacher who chooses homework assignments, important decisions are made at all levels of the organization on a daily, even hourly, basis. In reality, leaders who attempt to lead heroically reduce the effectiveness of their followers, over-burden themselves, and impair the organization's ability to respond adaptively to issues that may arise.

In contrast, *intensifying leadership* suggests that rather than focusing energy in one location or person, leadership is enhanced by the interaction and networking of many organizational members. By expanding the conception of who leads to include teachers, parents, and the wider community, schools have the potential to better meet the challenges they face. Intensifying leadership highlights the notion that leadership can be viewed as the intellectual and social outcomes of a group of *interacting individuals*. One prominent researcher likens this kind of leadership to a network of influence in which formal positions are less important than the belief by others that each person makes a difference (Spillane, Halverson, & Diamond, 2001). Another proponent of this perspective argues that the need for intensification demands a different "architecture" for school organizations that abandons the image of vertical authority (Gronn, 2000).

Rooted in communal action, intensified leadership suggests that when organizational members work in concert with each other they can pool their individual knowledge and expertise, resulting in better outcomes. Furthermore, intensified leadership is more than empowerment of individuals to complete specific tasks. The empowerment literature emphasizes the transfer of existing decision-making functions from school leaders to teachers through new special roles or structures in which teachers can exercise influence (Marks & Louis, 1997). While it is argued that sharing decision-making responsibility within the school will augment traditional leader influence, the size of the leadership pie usually remains the same. Intensified leadership opens the boundaries of leadership to include, in ongoing and permanent ways, a wide variety of members of the school and the surrounding community in new decision-making roles, and it asks them to become involved in generating new kinds of decisions and practices rather than simply carrying out existing functions. Jobs and roles are enlarged, and the range and type of decisions that can be made at all levels and by a variety of parties is increased. In this way, intensified leadership acknowledges that *expertise is distributed across the school organization and beyond*.

INTENSIFICATION AND BEYOND QUICK FIXES

We are familiar with the ways in which leaders can be seduced by the notion of a "quick fix" because we ourselves have held administrative positions (although not as principals). Opportunities to hear the latest expert abound; leadership and management texts offer appealing new insights and concepts. Methods for collecting and analyzing data roll out of state departments of education with alarming regularity. Technology is touted as the answer to the variety of instructional and leadership woes plaguing schools today. Furthermore, the pressure to raise test scores by the next test seems almost unbearable.

We sympathize with superintendents who ask for professional learning communities to be implemented in all buildings within the next month and arrange for a one-day workshop to ready the district. We understand why school principals use one-hour faculty meetings or single-day retreats to brainstorm about developing strategic plans designed to improve student achievement. We empathize with teachers who report that they intend to implement the new instructional practices but are observed to be lacking core skills to do so. We understand why schools hope that a good curriculum map inevitably will show the way to changes in classroom practice.

A good friend of ours refers to the smorgasbord of choices available to school leaders and teachers as "random acts of staff development" while another views both staff development and new policies as the "spray and pray" approach to school improvement. When people are frustrated and worried, they often look kindly at almost any idea that seems to have potential—or they may reject all ideas as "something we've tried before." When people feel discouraged and distracted, they hope that the additive quality of their efforts will create results. More often, the accumulated mountain of initiatives only leads to innovation fatigue.

However, we argue that, like the old adage, "if it seems too good to be true, it is," most new programs and staff development products won't take school leaders to the places they wish to go. Lasting change in school culture takes time, but without those changes, efforts to improve student learning are likely to be temporary. Real change in culture also requires more than time; it takes sustained effort focused on clearly understood and commonly shared goals and values. Embracing quick fixes fosters a belief in leaders that they are doing the best they can for the students in their schools. Instead, they often weaken the school culture's ability to engage in real change by nurturing pipe dreams. We shall explore briefly some of these false hopes.

1. Cultural change can occur quickly with new, enthusiastic leadership. As we have discussed, organizational cultures are deeply embedded in the practices and policies of the school. Though all members of a school organization might agree that change is needed, new and unproven policies and practices will be viewed skeptically. Even when cultures are viewed as negative, people would much rather "stay with what they know" than change. The insecurity of the unknown always makes the known a better bet. For these reasons, initiating cultural change is a slow, adaptive process.

2. Culture change can be stimulated from the outside through new policies. Inasmuch as culture is rooted in internal beliefs and values, it is resistant to external influence. Simply put, internal change may be stimulated from the outside, but it must be nurtured internally. State and even district policies lack the leverage and credibility to create the conditions of community, learning, and trust needed to foster real cultural change. This helps to account, of course, for the tangible variability in school cultures that often occur within any but the smallest districts. We are not arguing that districts and states have no influence on schools—there is plenty of evidence to indicate that they affect both practices and basic assumptions. However, more than policy or leadership change is needed for districts to have an impact on a school's culture (see Chapter 6).

3. Teachers and administrators should make the decisions—school culture should be dominated by professional values. An aspect we argue in more detail in Chapter 7 suggests that unless we engage the external school community in matters of school reform and innovation, schools cannot enjoy the broad support needed to be successful, nor are they fully capitalizing on their available resources. While schools may temporarily be able to insulate themselves from community pressures, they rely on establishing trusting relationships on an immediate practical level (voting for school funding). It is the longer-term impacts that are most important for this book: Schools that have trusting relationships with parents show greater student achievement gains according to a number of scholars (Bryk & Schneider, 2002). Developing shared values with the community, even when members of the community are of different races and have lower educational levels, is essential to creating supportive learning environments in the home and community.

4. More teamwork will create better school cultures. Clearly, teamwork matters. A hallmark of strong culture is communal activity toward shared goals. However, to mistake efforts to create teamwork for activities related to classroom teaching and learning activity is foolhardy. Teams can help to focus on the work creating improved outcomes for students, but they may also become competitive and distract teachers' attention from schoolwide goals and practices. Teams, like other school structures, need to be integrated into a network of relationships that may be less cohesive, but support a broader school improvement culture.

5. *Changing the school's mission and vision is the key to changing behavior and beliefs*. Missions can be motivating and introduce a new vocabulary and ideas to stimulate talk. Their impact on culture is often, however, limited to providing superficial understandings of complex ideas. When we adopt slogans about practice rather than real changes in practice, little changes. People's behavior and beliefs change when they engage in sustained learning that challenges their assumptions and provides better avenues to achieve results. As Peter Gronn pointed out some time ago, talking is at the center of this kind of administrative work. Leadership is exercised largely through informal communications rather than through significant decisions (Gronn, 1983). The centrality of sustained communication is emphasized by Schneider and Hollenczer (2006) as a critical tool in managing the simultaneous need for stability and fluidity, and managing the boundaries between external and internal pressures.

SUMMARY AND OVERVIEW OF THE BOOK

Culture change requires sustained effort, over a period of years, that is broadly distributed throughout a school and that centers on the combination of values and behaviors that allow teachers and administrators to make good choices during the very busy workdays that they always encounter. It requires spontaneous leadership actions as well as long-term strategic choices (more on this idea in Chapter 2); it requires the ability to address both the big picture and short-term demands simultaneously (more on this idea in Chapter 3). When schools attend to those aspects of their internal cultures that impede their ability to create community, learn together, and engender trust in each other, improvements in the outcomes for students are evident. But principals cannot do this alone or only in concert with the teachers in their building. The connections between leadership and culture change are further explored in Chapter 4. Principals also need colleagues and a professional network in which they can become reflective learners (more in Chapter 5); they need to be more strategic and effective in working with their district offices (Chapter 6), and in developing true partnerships with their parent and community stakeholders (Chapter 7). In Chapter 8 we return to our theme, and discuss how the themes and examples from the individual chapters are related to the work of school principals.

RECOMMENDED READINGS

Because this book is about leadership and change, we strongly recommend that you browse some of the following, which are among our favorites dealing with this topic. These books were selected because they contain durable ideas that will, especially if they are considered together, push almost anyone's ideas about change management beyond their current boundaries. In addition, they are all good reads and, though based in research, reflect an understanding of the problems of practice.

Bennis, W. (2000). *Managing the dream: Reflections on leadership and change.* New York: Perseus.

Every leader needs to be familiar with Warren Bennis, whose contributions to understanding modern organizations are without parallel. He is a former university president as well as a decades-long advisor to CEOs, and this book is a collection of some of his previously published writing on change.

Fullan, M. (1993). *Change forces: Probing the depths of educational reform.* New York: Falmer.

Michael Fullan is the foremost synthesizer of research on educational change. This book, which is the first (and we think still the best) of his series on change forces, outlines what we know about managing change in school settings. The second book, Change Forces: A Sequel, *and the third,* Change Forces With a Vengeance, *elaborate on the ideas presented in this early book, and are also worth looking at. This book is, however, the most practical, and if you haven't read it, you should!*

Hall, G., & Hord, S. (1987). *Change in schools: Facilitating the process.* Albany, NY: SUNY Press.

The authors of this book provide a useful theory of how individual change occurs during an organizational change effort. Their first perspective, Levels of Use, emphasizes the importance of gauging school-level change by understanding individual levels of familiarity and competence in taking on new behavior. The second perspective, Stages of Concern, looks at the emotional aspects of change. The models have been developed as both research and monitoring tools over many years, and are used throughout the world.

Kotter, J. P. (1996). *Leading change.* Boston: Harvard Business School Press.

John Kotter's book is one of the most popular among managers in the private sector. While not all business management texts are relevant to school administrators, this book provides an excellent overview of basic principles that we think are particularly relevant for principals. His discussion of how to generate "short-term wins" is an important antidote to long-term strategic plans that often weigh heavily on a tired change master.

Kouzes, J. M., & Posner, B. Z. (2002). *The leadership challenge.* San Francisco: Jossey-Bass.

This is a good companion book to Kotter's because we consider them the best of the popular general management books that emphasize the role of leadership in change. Clearly there are differences between business and school settings, but both of these books provide pointed summaries of what is known about strategic approaches to change. We particularly like Kotter's emphasis on how to provide a compelling vision for change and how to encourage people in the organization to come on board. Kouzes and Posner use their deep experience to succinctly outline the challenges of leadership, summarizing the qualities that help guide the personal traits that leaders must draw upon, and the way in which these qualities need to be expressed in order to motivate and encourage others. Both books focus on practices that can easily be adapted to educational settings.

Louis, K. S., & Miles, M. B. (1990). *Improving the urban high school: What works and why.* New York: Teachers College Press.

This is the only one of our recommended books that uses a lot of data—but it nevertheless develops a practical approach to managing the beginning stages of change when there are few resources, some hostile circumstances, and a sense of cynicism and fatigue among faculty members. While it is fifteen years old, the case studies of five high schools are not particularly dated.

Sarason, S. (1996). *Revisiting "The culture of the school and the problem of change."* New York: Teachers College Press.

This is a revision of Seymour Sarason's classic work on what needs to change in schools if student experiences and learning are to improve. Rather than looking at the quick fixes, Sarason concentrates on the basic features of school culture that make real change difficult. While this is not a quick read, it is essential for change masters who want to develop their own checklist of what needs to be altered in a school before significant change can occur. This is one of the few classic writings on change that pays a lot of attention to student experiences.

Schmoker, M. (1999). *Results: The key to continuous school improvement.* Arlington, VA: Association for Supervision and Curriculum Development.

This is the text for school leaders who want to understand what data-driven decision making can actually do for their schools. Mike Schmoker provides practical examples of what needs to happen before the school can become a real learning organization. His focus on using data positively is a welcome antidote to the sense that data are largely used to punish schools, teachers, and students.

Weick, K., & Sutcliffe, K. (2001). *Managing the unexpected: Assuring high performance in an age of complexity.* San Francisco: Jossey-Bass.

An invaluable tool for principals who are trying to create real change in classroom practices and student experiences, while at the same time working effectively within a results-based accountability environment. The emphasis on continuous improvement is a refreshing alternative to change management books that emphasize only transformation and "big, new thinking."

ANALYZING YOUR SCHOOL

Identifying Internal and External Foci

Consider the external and internal foci present in many schools. Identify how often each plays a role in your school. Then identify if this is work you are currently doing as an individual or as part of a leadership team. Circle those areas in which you might consider intensifying your leadership.

Internal Foci					
	Daily	*Weekly*	*Monthly*	*Individual*	*Team*
Student behavior and discipline					
Curriculum adoption and implementation					
Managing relationships with parents					
Managing faculty and staff relationships					
Budget and budget planning					
School improvement and change agendas					
Vision and mission setting					
Accountability and testing					
Scheduling and building operations					
Supervision and coaching					
Planning for professional development					
External Foci					
Community contacts and relationships focused on issues or events within the school					
District office meetings					
Participation in district office initiatives					
Networking with other professionals					
Countywide or regional meetings					
Working with community groups on non–school-related issues					
Working with social workers or community health professionals					

2

Principals as Cultural Change Agents

In this chapter we focus on the role of leadership in developing school culture. As we noted in Chapter 1, intensified leadership includes broadening the meaningful involvement of others in the leadership process *and* the deepening of one's thinking about the large goals and small tasks that comprise the day-to-day work in schools. We will distinguish between management and leadership and develop understandings related to the aspects of each that contribute to positive school cultures.

In this chapter you will:

- be introduced to the role of school leaders in developing school culture;
- identify the most significant educational subcultures that need your attention; and
- understand the difference and overlap between leadership and management and how each is important in developing school cultures.

Think for a minute about a leader you admire. Now think about what aspects of his or her leadership you find compelling. You might recall a favorite teacher, remembering how he or she could lead a class in understanding difficult and challenging material. That teacher may have clearly explained the processes required in solving a tricky computation or perhaps could make historical figures come alive through carefully crafted stories and examples. Instead, you might recall a coach, someone who motivated you to achieve beyond that which you thought you were capable. Finally, you might think of a business leader or politician, remembering his savvy choice or her ability to bring a crowd to its feet. In any case, leaders are remembered, and respected, for the ways in which they approach people and problems.

We ascribe greatness to leaders for their handling of extraordinary situations. Most of us, however, have few experiences with situations that require definitive action to preserve a group. Instead, our lives are made up of small, incremental decision opportunities that present themselves every day. Separately, each incident might not seem important, but how we approach these daily tasks matters. Furthermore, how we approach a given situation matters as much as what we do. Consider the following:

TWO LEADERS, THE SAME TASK, DIFFERENT STRATEGIES

Tom Cook has been an assistant principal for curriculum and instruction at Harris Primary School for more than five years. Primarily responsible for teacher evaluation and the alignment of teachers' lessons with state standards, Cook is a regular visitor to classrooms. He describes his job this way: "I'm the enforcer. It's my job to work within the system and to be sure the entire curriculum gets covered and that the standards get taught. I schedule 'rounds' of the classrooms. I like to think of myself like a doctor, going around to each classroom, kind of like taking the temperature of the building. Every day, I check where the teachers are against our curriculum pacing guides. . . . They are required to turn in their lesson plans to my office every week. Then, I try to reach every classroom, every day. . . . I write notes to the teachers about how they're progressing. I usually get a note to every teacher about once a week. If I see someone falling behind, I make extra effort to check to see if there is anything they need to catch up." He pauses and adds, "Sometimes it's exhausting. I'm in the classrooms so much I don't really have time to do the other things I wish I had time to do. I just keep up."

Jolene Wilson is also an assistant principal in the same district as Cook, but at McKinley Elementary. Though their job descriptions are identical, she approaches her work quite differently. She explains, "Bottom line—my job is to get the standards taught. The district has these pacing guides but I don't worry about them so much. I worry more about what the kids are learning and how we know they're learning it. Our contract requires teachers to turn in their lesson plans each week but I make my teachers turn in their plan *and* the assignments they're giving to the kids. I want teachers to make sure the kids know the material before they move on. If the kids bomb their homework or a test and it takes an extra day to be sure they all get something, that's okay. I let them know that if they need to skip some stuff, I'll support them." She adds, "I know I'm not in classrooms as much as some people. . . . I spend my time going to grade-level meetings and working with teachers on their assignments and assessments. For me that's what matters. When teachers talk with each other about how they are teaching, everyone gets better at it. I figure quality matters; I work on getting what happens in classrooms to be quality."

When we interviewed teachers at both Harris and McKinley, Cook and Wilson were described by teachers in similar ways. Of Cook, a third-grade teacher said: "He's great at what he does for us. I stay to the pacing guide because of him, but that's not a bad thing. For the first time in my career I feel like someone cares enough to know what is happening in my classroom." When speaking about Wilson, a fifth-grade teacher commented, "She really cares. She understands what I deal with every day and what it takes to do this job. I've had to change a lot of what I used to do; I'm a better teacher for what she's made us do." In short, both were described as caring, focused individuals who support teachers in trying to achieve student learning goals. Each has earned the trust of teachers and spends considerable time working on the district's objective—ensuring that the standards were taught in all classrooms. In both schools, overall test scores have risen, average yearly progress has been made, and faculty turnover rates have decreased.

It is "safer" to be a Tom Cook than a Jolene Wilson, because Jolene has to place more trust in her teachers. However, Jolene loves her job, and Tom is perennially exhausted. We argue that their approach to the work of creating a strong culture promoting student learning is qualitatively different in ways that go beyond their job satisfaction. Cook keeps the school on track by *personally* ensuring that curriculum and instructional standards are met, but in that process stretches himself to the point where he can do little else. In contrast, Wilson is engaged in the process of *leading the faculty* toward a collective responsibility for refining the curriculum and their instructional practices. Rather than being an "enforcer" of requirements or a "doctor" with treatments for ailing classrooms, she stimulates the teachers to create their own improvement in the instructional program.

In other words, although both leaders appear on the surface to be involved with similar practices that result in similar outcomes, we argue that Wilson approaches her work in a way that is inducing important cultural changes. By placing student learning instead of compliance with district policies at the heart of her work, she encourages teachers to consider new practices and supports experimentation in meaningful ways. We believe that the distinction between administrative behaviors that *maintain* the organization (generally thought of as management behaviors) versus those that *stimulate* the organization to change its ways of doing business (generally considered leadership behaviors) is important. The culture of the school is influenced by these choices and, in the long run, we have accumulated data that link these changes to increased student learning and achievement.

CULTURES AND SUBCULTURES IN SCHOOLS

It is often assumed that a school has a singular or dominant culture. That is, of course, true in some cases, particularly in smaller schools located in relatively homogeneous communities. One example is the common finding that new charter schools have more agreement among teachers (who were recruited to the school knowing what its values represent),

Figure 2.1   Subcultural Arenas in Schools

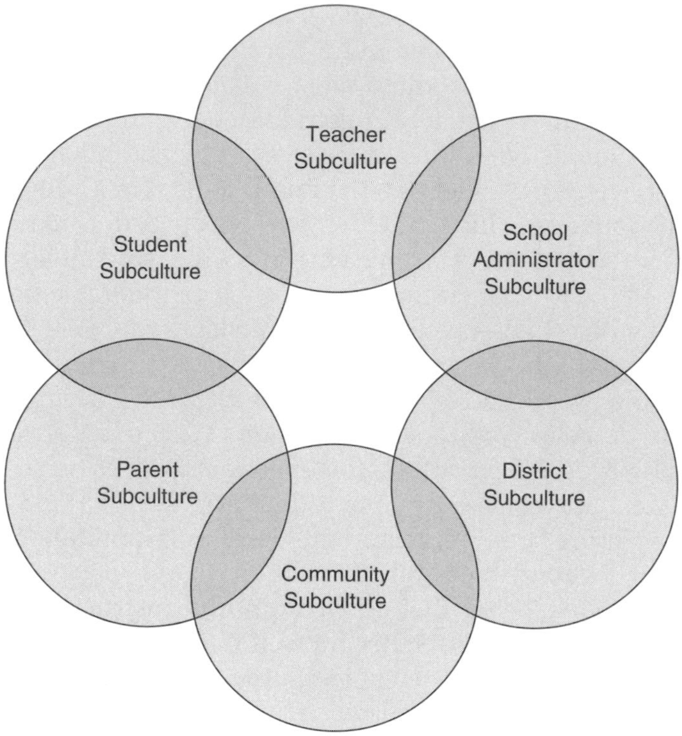

administrators (who are usually involved in setting the initial directions and curriculum), and parents (who often do more "research" about the school before choosing to move their children from a previous setting).

Most schools are not, however, blessed with the conditions that foster such cohesiveness. Instead, the real life of schools is usually characterized by the coexistence of multiple cultures that accommodate each other but are not the same. Six overlapping but distinct subcultures, each characterized by its own preferences, values, and expectations, are immediately apparent to anyone who has spent much time in schools (Figure 2.1).

Three professional subcultures stand out in Figure 2.1. Outsiders may talk about the "local school system" but insiders are acutely aware of the differences between them. Within the school, *teacher subcultures* usually focus on managing the daily task of engaging a large number of students in learning activities in individual classrooms. Even in a large departmentalized high school, the teacher subculture usually has a number of consistent expectations and norms; for example, that administrators should take care of unusually disruptive students and insulate teachers from parent and community demands that interfere with classroom routines (Rossmiller, 1992). Our complex figure doesn't take into account that in larger schools there are often subcultures within the teacher subculture.

A *school administrator subculture* consists of the norms and expectations held by members of the leadership team about how the school should be managed, and who in the school should do what. An example is the usual assumption in middle and high schools that student discipline should be assigned primarily to one person. Another traditional belief is that the administrative team is responsible for policy, while teachers are responsible for the curriculum. In most cases, the school administrator subculture is distinct from a *district subculture,* which focuses on managing several schools and creating policies that will adjudicate between individual school cultures and community and legal and/or state expectations. Examples of differences in perspectives between schools and the district office are everywhere in the educational literature, often highlighting the tension between district efforts to standardize procedures and program, and the desire of schools to maintain their own ways of doing things.

There are also three subcultures that are composed of nonprofessionals, with different stakes in the operation of the schools. Since the 1930s, sociologists have discovered (and rediscovered) an independent *student subculture* that is focused on maximizing social engagement and minimizing adult control (Waller, 1932). Even among very young children, the emergence of social groupings that undermine the preferences of teachers can be observed (Corsaro, Molinari, Hadley, & Sugioka, 2003), and in secondary schools, distinctive student subcultures (e.g., jocks, nerds, burnouts) may conflict with adult subcultures in different ways. *Parent subcultures* influence children, but parents also have their own formally and informally organized ways of working with the schools that their children attend, and it is common knowledge among educators that parent relations in schools with an active upper middle-class PTA are very different than those in schools in which parents are working several jobs to make ends meet (Lareau & Horvat, 1999). Parents are members of the community, but their subculture in oriented to getting the most for their own children, while the broader *community subculture* may not have the same values and objectives. For example, in communities where many parents choose private education, support for public schools (and the willingness to vote for bond issues) may be lower, while criticism is higher (Sikkink, 1999).

In recent years, school administrators have been urged to spend their time primarily on being "instructional leaders." Figure 2.1 suggests, however, that this is unrealistic: A principal can't ignore the other subcultures, because they are part of the daily demands facing school administrators. To the extent that these subcultures are distant or in conflict with one another, they create many unavoidable distractions from the goal of instructional leadership, but they cannot be ignored because the members of the subculture have a legitimate interest the school. If the principal sees his or her job as holding students' and outsiders' demands at bay so that teachers can focus on their work, they are engaging in the Sisyphean task of pushing a boulder up a hill, only to have it fall back every night.

In the best of all possible worlds, the principal will *manage and lead the groups toward a greater consensus* (or at least an accommodation) as part of the effort to intensify leadership. If the principal is successful, Figure 2.1 might look more like Figure 2.2, where there is more cultural overlap, indicating strong areas of agreement that can serve as a basis for cultural change. In schools with substantial overlap, where the culture is mutually understood and accepted, there is less conflict, more participation in decision making and other leadership initiatives and, generally, more agreement on directions and choices. However, substantial cultural overlap does not insure schools against the complexity of school improvement and reform efforts. Even when members of the school community agree on directions and means to attain goals, maintaining positive and productive school cultures is the result of consistent and deliberate leadership effort.

A simple example of a high school that recently developed a student uniform policy suggests how this works. When teachers in Valleyfield High (which will reappear in Chapter 3) complained about having to monitor baggy pants worn too low and revealing cleavage, the administrators convened a group to develop a uniform policy. Parents, students, and teachers were represented. Parents in this low-income school were concerned about

Figure 2.2   Subcultural Arenas in Schools—With Overlap

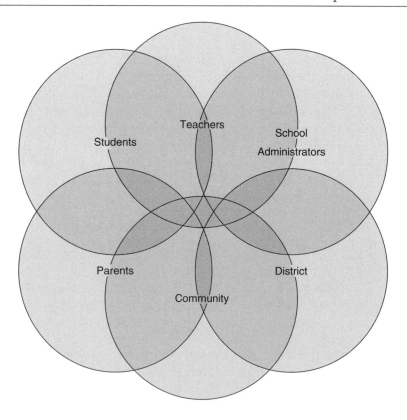

the cost of regulation uniforms, students about fashion, and teachers about consistency. The "uniform" that resulted was simple: black pants; grey shirts with collars, tucked in; and no hats or large jewelry. Parents were pleased because they could buy their clothes at Kmart and save money, students voted for a code that was consistent with the style preferred by many of the students, and teachers felt that they had gotten a "uniform" that had no relationship to gang colors. The school leader's role was to ensure that the group met until they had reached consensus.

MANAGEMENT AND LEADERSHIP

When we have argued that school administrators need to manage and lead toward more consistency, we use the words *manage* and *lead* deliberately. Over the past fifty years, the terms have often been used interchangeably, but confusion and disagreement currently reign. When a distinction is made between them in the popular management literature, it is often simplistic, such as the "difference between being a manager and being a leader is simple. Management is a career. Leadership is a calling," (Kossoff, n.d.) or the modern-day proverb, "leadership is about doing the right thing; management is about doing things right." Leadership scholars tend to take a more nuanced position, but some business-school gurus have endowed the idea of leadership with an almost priestlike quality, equating it with visioning, creating, proselytizing, designing anew (bricolage), and divining (Westley & Mintzberg, 1989), thus suggesting that management is what is left over.

Uncertainty surrounding the terms is compounded by the fact that some prominent researchers suggest that leadership and management are qualitatively different and mutually exclusive constructs (Bennis & Nanus, 2003), while others view each as addressing distinctly different goals and outcomes for the organization with some complementary and overlapping skill sets (Kotter, 1996). In the educational literature, much has also been made of this distinction, suggesting that whether the principal leads or maintains the school can provide noteworthy insight into a school's effectiveness (Leithwood, Leonard, & Sharratt, 1998).

The problem with the current emphasis on leadership and its differentiation from management is that there are simply not enough saviors to staff ailing businesses and schools. We believe, based on our observations of school leaders, that distinctions should be made—we think that the differences in the way that Tom Cook and Jolene Wilson approached their district's increased efforts to align and be accountable for the curriculum is a good example. We reject, however, anointing "leaders" with superpowers and "managers" with plodding diligence. We prefer the approach taken by those who suggest that both are needed, that they coexist and are, in observable practice, often indistinct (Senge, 2002; Yukl, 2002).

Embedded in this argument is the notion that making a school hum requires the skill of a strong leader and a highly competent manager—usually wrapped up in the same individual or at least present within the same team. The distinction suggests that we are concerned both with organizational functions typically attributed to *leadership*—working on sustained system improvement, enticing and empowering staff to achieve top performances, and developing trust within the organization—as well as with organizational functions typically credited to *management*—working within the system, organizing regularized and predictable operations and supervising the performance of staff.

In particular, we argue that schools are settings that require administrators to address daily operations and long-term adaptive planning and vision simultaneously. As a consequence, they must be prepared to

Figure 2.3   Management and Leadership in School Administration

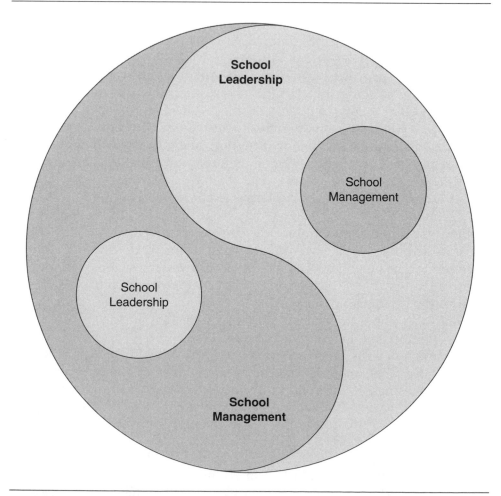

SOURCE: Adapted from M. Schratz. (2003). From administering to leading a school. *Cambridge Journal of Education, 33*(3), 408.

manage *and* lead—often in the same meeting and with the same people. Furthermore, the challenges of school leadership include daily problem solving and decision making, as well as incorporating long-term planning and situational adjustments as need arises. In this way, management and leadership are not distinctive but blend almost seamlessly in practice. One of our colleagues has proposed an analogy to the familiar yin-yang figure, in which the dualistic principles of masculine and feminine are tempered by inclusion of a seed of the feminine within the masculine and vice versa (Schratz, 2003). We show our version of it in Figure 2.3. The important feature of this schematic is that leadership and management contain each other, even though we can see and describe examples of how they are different, as well as making definitional distinctions.

When leadership is exhibited within areas typically focused on daily management tasks, principals are often less visible; the example of the Valleyfield uniform policy is a clear example. In this case, leadership involved structuring opportunities for others within the school to take on new roles. By including others, the school's capacity for problem solving increases and learning is enhanced. Management is important in leadership activities, such as setting new directions for school improvement. Preparing people for effective change requires, for example, that teachers have access to professional development when they need it rather than when it fits into the existing calendar. Leaders must attend to the schedule, the availability of appropriate support and resources, and other details that, if mismanaged, can diminish teacher confidence.

What can we see when we look at a school where administrators are doing both, and who, at the same time, engage professional colleagues and others with a clear stake in school success? We see individuals and administrative teams that:

- focus on stimulating, energizing, and coordinating professional activity within the school;
- span boundaries to include external stakeholders to build support and gather resources for student learning;
- create an environment of mutual responsibility and accountability for supporting students and creating change;
- build links between older practices and ways of thinking and the future;
- develop professional community and organizational learning with the specific intention of changing their school culture;
- sustain a vision of schooling that emphasizes dignity and changing lives;
- adopting an attitude of *serving* as well as *doing*; and
- remain focused on long-term strategic goals while attending to the daily tasks and activities that ensure smooth operations.

This is a long list of tasks. Which of these are management and which are leadership? In Figure 2.4 we have organized them within the same

Figure 2.4 Cultural Management and Leadership in Schools

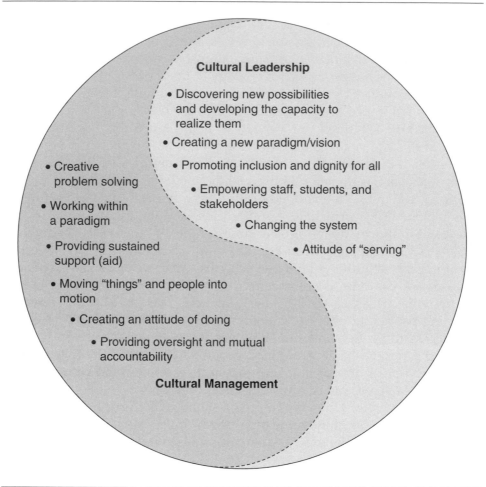

SOURCE: Adapted from M. Schratz. (2003). From administering to leading a school. *Cambridge Journal of Education, 33*(3), 408.

yin-yang diagram that we presented in Figure 2.3, but have changed the dividing line between the two halves to a dotted one to emphasize their interconnections. In the chapters that follow, we provide numerous examples of how principals in real schools have addressed them.

Can one person or even a small team do all of these things every day? Clearly not, except in the most extraordinary cases. Erecting an ideal that simply can't be met begs the observer to mutter "yeah, sure . . ." and return to doing things in the same old way—there is not enough time and not enough resources. The only way that this agenda can be carried out is to intensify leadership so that responsibility for developing and maintaining a vital school culture is widely shared among all of the stakeholders. This means, of course, that more people need to be brought into the

leadership arena—which also means that the image of the school administrator as the "buck-stops-here kind of guy (or gal)" needs to radically
shift. As the tasks of leadership and management become more blurred,
opportunities to intensify leadership abound. If attending to the complexity of these issues is too much for one person—and we believe that it is—
then school leaders must look to others to carry out these roles.

Anders Elementary, where a site-based team has been in place since
the late 1960s, offers one example of how attention to intensified leadership can enhance success.

ANDERS ELEMENTARY AND SITE-BASED MANAGEMENT (SBM)

When it was first founded, the Anders SBM team offered input to the principal concerning
decisions regarding the school. As district and state accountability pressures grew, the team
developed a larger role, reviewing the yearly test reports, coordinating staff development,
and pressing for strategic goals focused on changed classroom practice. Principal Martinez
calls the team his "better brain." He explains, "It's too hard to do it any other way. I can't
tell the teachers to do this or that. They need to decide the best choice. We have to work
together. We can't have people going in different directions. We can't afford sloppy thinking. We have to stick together for the kids. The only way I can say it is we lead together."
Martinez has increased the number of players able to respond when need arises, but the
team does not simply wait for an issue to present itself. Instead, it is seen by all as setting
the tone for expectations of professional behavior and practice.

Developing SBM teams offers principals straightforward ways to
intensify leadership efforts. An easygoing man, Principal Martinez had no
problems putting data on the table and asking for help. He prided himself
on his openness to and belief in his staff's ability to effectively identify and
solve problems. But many principals still struggle when asked to share
their hard-earned authority, particularly when they have worked for a
long time in systems that reward a "line management" approach.

DEVELOPING A SITE COUNCIL AT DANE MIDDLE SCHOOL

Gene Goldberg was the kind of principal who took satisfaction in being the "first one in
and the last one out" of the building every day. As he put it, "I want my teachers to know
I'm here for them. I want the kids and parents to be able to find me if they need
something. I like being the face of Dane. That's why I became a principal." But as he
neared the end of his tenth year, he noted that his job had changed: "Used to be that

(Continued)

(Continued)

I mostly walked the building and knew what was happening.... But now I spend more time worried about meeting the benchmarks and indicators.... Before, it was me. If things were good, I was proud; if we had problems, I worked to solve them. Now I need other people to make all this happen." In an effort to foster increased accountability, Goldberg formed "the council," whose membership includes teachers and also three parents. Charged with student learning as its core goal, the council addresses everything from professional development to student behavior. As one parent said, "If it has the potential to have anything to do with learning, we talk about it." At first, this was difficult for Goldberg: "I didn't want our dirty laundry on the table. But then I realized they (the parents) knew most of it anyway. Man it was hard."

   As the council evolved, so did Goldberg. As a teacher bluntly put it, "Gene was a great guy, but sort of a good old boy. You could count on him to back you but... he wasn't real attuned to what was in classrooms." She credits the council with a "major turnaround. It used to be all about him.... The focus has changed to *us* and we're not going back."

In many ways, Dane Middle School exemplifies the best of intensified leadership efforts. By spanning boundaries between the old hierarchy of administration and teachers and parents, the council has created an atmosphere of mutual responsibility for student success. Change is supported and communal learning is encouraged. The day-to-day tasks of running the school are addressed while the wider goals are an ongoing point of discussion. People at Dane observed that culture had radically changed as a result of intensification. The Anders and Dane experiences suggest that that cultural management and leadership in schools is a process that requires leaders to change, even if it is uncomfortable. It requires that the traditional idea of *who* leads be thoughtfully considered within the context of the school. We turn now discussing the other side of this equation: *what* is being lead.

PATHS TO CULTURAL MANAGEMENT AND LEADERSHIP

We have established that there are at six important groups that need to be brought into the cultural leadership and management equation, we have shown that leadership and management involve overlapping but distinctive work on the part of school administrators, and we know from the previous chapter that managing and leading culture requires targeting three critical components of school culture: professional community, organizational learning, and trust. But identifying key groups and cultural arenas shouldn't necessarily lead to a one-size-fits-all approach to how to work with them, or the strategies that you might use to create intensified leadership. Two further complications are necessary preconditions for beginning a diagnosis of your school's cultural strengths and needs: Who should be involved in what as leadership is intensified, and what local conditions will affect your work in leadership intensification. As we develop these ideas, we will draw on the example of Metro High School's path to change.

METRO HIGH'S PATH TO CHANGE

Housed in an old building, Metro stood out only because of its occasionally winning basketball team. Graduation rates were average, student performance on state-level tests was within acceptable ranges, and the school had few major disciplinary events. While other schools within the district regularly made the front page of the local section for remarkable theater programs or difficulties with drugs and violence, Metro flew under the radar of most within the city. Teachers taught and students learned (or didn't). Departments met quarterly, but conversation was more perfunctory than philosophical. District officials paid little attention, knowing that although Metro certainly wasn't a star, it wasn't an ongoing problem either. Unlike school improvement stories that begin with great fanfare, many can't specify how they began the process that resulted in change. Some credit early progress on efforts to increase the number of students passing the tenth-grade graduation test. Some credit a group of teachers who attended a writing workshop in 1999. Still others claim they "just got tired of how it used to be."

Who Should Be Involved?

The old assumptions about the role of principals as protectors of the core functions of classroom teaching are not all wrong. Any principal who has had to deal with an overly demanding parent, or the requests by a district office to initiate an instructional program that would disrupt successful change efforts already under way in the school, knows that he or she must play an important role in managing the boundaries of the school. While there are no hard-and-fast rules, we argue that it is helpful to look at the three components of culture as nested, with the core (professional community) being most clearly dominated by the staff within the school; organizational learning, involving greater participation by students, the district office, and community members; and trust, requiring equal engagement of all partners. A visual depiction of what we have in mind is presented in Figure 2.5.

Professional community, which lies at the center of the figure, requires that teachers have a protected environment in which they can honestly and openly discuss their practice, a place in which small failures are acceptable, and conversations focus on what teachers are doing to ensure that all students are learning. It also lies at the core of organizational learning and

Figure 2.5   Layers of School Culture

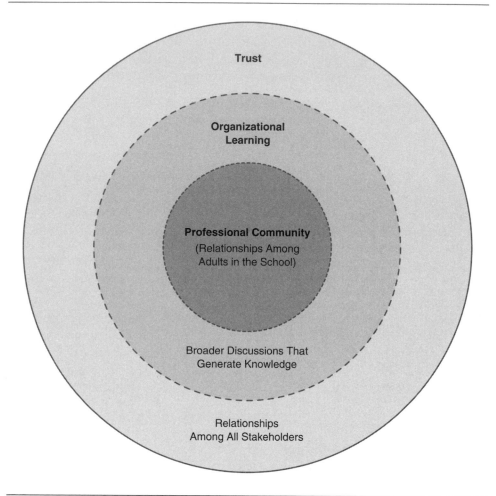

is a necessary foundation for trust. However, as a number of authors have pointed out, professional communities should be restricted, but not closed. A recent study of professional community in England found, for example, that the most successful schools incorporated paraprofessionals (Bolam, Stoll, & Greenwood, 2007), while others have advocated for the inclusion of counselors and social workers in deeper conversations about supporting student learning (Louis & Gordon, 2006). These changes in how teachers work with each other and with the school community are unlikely to occur without active leadership. Many teachers report, for example, that they are willing to seek collegial advice because their principal advocates and supports risk taking. The process must also be managed, however, because without active efforts to get groups of teachers (teams, grade-level groups, departments, etc.) to talk to each other, a school can easily become balkanized into insular and even competitive groups (Kruse & Louis, 1997).

EMERGING PROFESSIONAL COMMUNITY IN METRO HIGH

A group of ninth-grade teachers met with the principal to request support for attending a workshop on writing across the curriculum. They returned to Metro excited to incorporate the ideas they learned and began by adding a writing component to their course each week. In October 1998, the English and social studies teachers created an assignment in which students who were enrolled in both their classes could receive credit for the work in both classes—the history content was given a history grade and the English content a separate score.

Not surprisingly, this was popular among students, who preferred one longer assignment to two shorter ones. The two teachers saw the effort as evidence that they could engage student's interest in more complex work while at the same time increasing the quality of what they turned in. Buoyed by their success, the pair began a regular practice of coupling assignments. As registration for spring semester neared, savvy students began to lobby the guidance counselors for schedule changes that allowed them to enroll in the paired courses. Interested, the guidance team met with the teachers, and it was agreed to add additional sections in the fall.

The shifts in the fall schedule piqued the school's interest, and in early February the principal met with the team to see if there was anything more he might do for them. They declined, saying they were doing just fine as long as he'd "keep letting us do what we were doing." They did, however request that they be assigned to work together in the following school year, and proposed a pilot program that would allow them to integrate writing across all their courses. They offered to take 100 kids randomly and to work with the guidance office to minimize disruption in scheduling. During the 2000–2001 school year, the program took root. The teachers were not shy about their efforts and invited as many other teachers as wanted to observe, while working with a small tenth-grade team to adopt the paired assignment process.

The example of Metro High shows how the principal can be central yet largely invisible in a change process. In Metro, he played an important role by his initial willingness to invest limited school resources in the workshop, and continued his support by making sure that other faculty members didn't feel threatened by the activities of the ninth-grade teachers. By keeping up to date on what was being done by the teachers, he continued to provide encouragement.

The case also illustrates the importance of having an open professional community environment. The innovating team made sure that the counselors were actively involved so that their program wouldn't become a scheduling burden, and engaged them in discussions about how to make the traditionally difficult ninth-grade experience a successful one. They were open with other teachers—they shared, didn't preach, and those who wished to learn more found them easy to work with.

While schools usually have many teachers who actively seek out individual learning opportunities (like the ninth-grade teachers at Metro), it is rarer to find schools where individual learning is incorporated into on-going reflection. A traditional role of principals is to serve as a "gate-keeper" who determines what information is worth discussing more broadly (Wahlstrom & Louis, 1993). But under today's conditions and demands for rapid change, the role of gatekeeper must shift to promoting freer consideration of new ideas. This requires both leadership (to encourage and promote individuals to seek ideas) and management (providing opportunities within the school day and year for sharing and discussion).

METRO HIGH LEARNS TO LEARN

As the paired assignment practices slowly gained momentum, the counseling office became more involved both with scheduling courses so students could couple their learning and by encouraging students to consider the option in their schedule. More and more paired assignments were created and teachers began sharing them. Over several iterations the assignments became more polished. By the end of the 2004–2005 school year, paired assignments were in place either formally (in teams where students were purposefully enrolled) or informally (in classes where teachers made the practice an option for students) across more than two-thirds of the building for at least one assignment each semester.

The payoff for teachers was largely in seeing student performance on their classroom assignment soar. As one teacher commented, "By doing this we are clear with kids about what we expect. They can't say, 'Miss Jones, don't make me do it' because I know better. I know that assignment. I know the expectation and I tell them that." Another teacher noted, "It's easy. It gives them practice on the stuff that is on the test . . . just this way it's better." For many teachers, the collective aspect of the innovation was important because it has led to broader discussions about improving the school, As one teacher stated, "It gives us something to talk about at department meetings that gets us going on all sorts of stuff—talking to parents and what you're going to teach next." This teacher added a common sentiment that the collective learning was empowering: "It's a way I feel like what I do matters around here. Like someone is interested in what I think."

Trusting relationships inside the school, such as those built at Metro, are a foundation, and they allowed the principal to maintain overall responsibility for the change effort while giving teachers the freedom to design and carry out the work. His practice was to check in frequently, to make sure that everyone was still on track, and to support what he saw as an important effort for the school.

We know that teachers who don't trust their students also don't obtain good learning results, and that teachers who don't trust each other don't share innovative practices. But student-teacher trust must also include the development of trust with parents and with the community at large. Where parents and communities don't trust their schools, resources inevitably will decline, and students increasingly will be drawn to alternatives, including charter schools and home instruction. While principals cannot make people trust one another, they provide important examples of promoting openness and dialogue. In addition, principals may play a critical role in cementing trusting relationships between the school and the district, by being modest about successes and failures. The Metro High story shows that trust between schools and their outside stakeholders can take some time to build.

METRO HIGH—A LEADER IN THE DISTRICT?

During this time, the principal at Metro retired, and the district named one of the existing assistant principals to the lead role. When in spring 2006 the district announced that it was planning on adopting the practice of common assessments across similar courses in high schools, the new principal stepped forward, claiming, "We've done this already." At the end of the 2006–2007 year, it was announced that the Metro staff was to lead district teams in designing common assessments.

The Metro High story is an example of how intensified leadership can create real changes in a school's culture over time, and at the same time creates the foundation for improved student learning. Teachers' engagement in meaningful professional development activated critical reflection upon their practice. Individually, their sense of professionalism was reinforced by collegial interaction and challenge. As trust grew, so did teachers' willingness to share the knowledge that improved their practice. The early involvement of counselors ensured that potential roadblocks in scheduling never arose. Collectively, the faculty created and shared norms of practice based on an unremitting emphasis on producing evidence of student learning. Overall professionalism increased, not because of formalized programs and policies but rather because teachers worked together to identify problems of practice and address them through ongoing discussions about their work.

Furthermore, the principal in this scenario fostered cultural change largely by managing the existing system to support teachers' efforts. He and the new principal were instrumental in creating a culture within the school that was based on mutual trust and respect. His instructional leadership was indirect, by shaping the routines that kept Metro High School operating smoothly while making space for a major innovation in teacher practice. His steady relationships with the community and parents ensured that there was no conflict over more demanding assignments or less homework. When offered the opportunity to support a "bottom-up" effort he grasped for it, but his pressure on the team was limited to keeping track of what they were doing on a regular basis. In other words, he managed the existing culture effectively, and his subtle leadership role emphasized empowering others and providing dignity and choice to staff and students. He exemplified servant leadership during a period of change.

The Ever-Changing Conditions That Shape School Culture

Metro High School, as all schools, exists in a specific context. In the case of Metro, conditions aligned to allow for intensified leadership to flourish. However, we emphasize that school cultures, and the assumptions and values held by the six different subgroups, are shaped by variable and fluid conditions that need to be factored into the daily work of school administrators.

Many of these are familiar to any principal who has completed the required courses for administrative licensure because they parallel the chapters or headings in administration textbooks. Among these are external factors (e.g., demographics, the local school finance situation, local and national governmental accountability requirements) as well as issues internal to the school itself (such as staff and faculty recruitment and retention). We shall briefly discuss some of those that we think are most important for a principal to keep in mind, and emphasize how they intersect with leading and managing a school's culture.

Geography and Demographics

Schools are deeply connected with their community and attendance areas served by the school. The hopes and values that characterize a school's community affect almost every aspect of educators' daily work, whether or not they are conscious of it. Relationships with parents are a constant source of stress for most schools, in part because schools are often poorly equipped to communicate effectively with their primary stakeholders. Relationships between professional educators and parents revolve around two key issues: the demand for parental voice and the demand for the "adequate, fair, and appropriate" distribution of educational services. Our work suggests that the more school leaders seek to increase the connection between the school and the real world the greater the relationship between public support for and of the school. As a consequence, we devote Chapter 7 to this condition.

Financial Stability

Schools depend on public financing, but in most cases face increasing pressures to increase efficiency. Broadly defined, efficiency refers to the act of minimizing inputs (local and state dollars) while maximizing outputs and gains (student achievement and success). Simply put, efficiency suggests that school leaders need to find ways to do more with less. In addition to technical issues concerning tax burdens and revenue distribution, financial demands are usually a reflection of the community's focus on defining *what* schools (and educational leaders) will be held accountable for and *how* this accountability will be assessed. If school administrators treat the dialogue around finance as merely a matter of dollars and cents, they miss the subtext of the conversation, which is on the larger community's expectations for the school.

Governmental Accountabilities

Schools cannot avoid the multiple levels of formal accountability that drive the internal life of schools, from the mountains of paperwork to the annual report cards that appear in the local newspapers and on state Web sites. Educators are now preoccupied with federal requirements for testing, teacher qualifications, and disaggregated achievement data, but these are merely layered on to the demands that educators have come to take for granted, ranging from various state mandates, program guidelines, shifting civil rights and equity requirements, and special court orders, among others. The threat of lawsuits has a longer history than concern about becoming a "failing school" under No Child Left Behind legislation, but both induce anxiety and occasional timidity among those who work in schools. What educators often fail to note, however, is that mandates and legal requirements typically occur in areas in which there is emerging or already strong cultural consensus that "things need to change." While it is easily argued that government mandates and accountability hinder schools' progress toward important goals, our work suggests that administrators who remain focused on the underlying messages—the expectations that schools will improve learning for all students—have found increased accountability to be less of a burden.

Internal Conditions Affecting School Culture

In our discussion of the cases introduced in this chapter, we have already suggested many conditions that support the growth of positive school cultures. The example of Metro High, for example, allows us to see the importance of developing community, learning, and trust, as well as leadership that supports improvement efforts. However, our research suggests that other circumstances also have the potential to affect cultural change within schools. These include the following.

Shared Norms and Values

Without a core of shared beliefs about institutional purposes, practices, and desired behavior, school cultures devoted to organizational improvement and change cannot emerge. Even if teachers want to form more cohesive social and professional relations, the absence of a shared understanding of "what we believe" and "how we contribute to this school" instead will produce mistrust and conflict. This does not mean that teachers must unthinkingly embrace a "party line" (which, as we discuss elsewhere in this book, does little to affect lasting cultural change), but it does mean that considerable time and effort must be devoted to supporting school members in efforts to delineate that which they wish to become. Shared norms and values are not usually the same as a mission statement, which reflects a compact public declaration about a school's purpose rather than the detailed, usually unwritten, and highly complex set of understandings about "how we work together in this school" to achieve the mission.

Skill and Will

It is obvious that without the knowledge and skills, change will not occur. Equally obvious is the observation that without a uniformly strong level of commitment to action, efforts at cultural change will fall on stony soil (Miles & Louis, 1990). Most change efforts, however, fail due to an absence of one or both of these factors. The lack of skills needed to implement new programs causes teachers and principals to give up, blaming failure on the program's inability to deliver on its promise rather than looking internally for a cause. School leaders must be particularly active in anticipating the mismatch between what people want to do and what they are able to do. Knowing how to collaborate, how to structure decision-making opportunities, and how to use data in problem solving and decision making are skills that leaders need to learn, model, and facilitate in others. Equally damaging is an absence of will. We define will as a person's or organization's determination and commitment to move toward a stated goal or vision. In demonstrating will, school leaders generate energy and excitement for the project in which they engage and motivate others to join them in their quest. While knowledge and skill are more information dependent, willpower can be generated by the investment of leaders in the ability of school members to advance.

Staff and Faculty Turnover

Many studies indicate that staff stability is a minimal condition for developing a positive school culture and promoting student learning. All too often the wind goes out of important projects when key personnel retire or leave. Efforts to connect with the larger community can be undermined when trusted associates and friends leave their positions. When teacher teams have new members every year, it is almost impossible to establish the smooth working relationships required to make collaborative work a pleasure rather than a chore. While turnover can hinder improvement efforts, our own and other's research suggests a vibrant school culture is one that supports recruitment and retention of the best teachers so that the few "retired in place" issues that inevitably arise can be dealt with in humane and respectful ways.

Environmental Turbulence

Environmental turbulence refers to the amount of change and complexity in the environment that surrounds the school, and can result from the effects of one or more of the factors discussed above. The greater the amount of change in environmental factors, such as those discussed above about regulations, the higher the level of environmental turbulence. Generally, environmental turbulence is difficult for schools because it increases the vulnerability of the school organization to disruptions of the system. Whether a levy fails or a new superintendent is appointed, turbulence within the environment causes leaders to address the interplay between older, institutionalized activities with new demands and stresses.

CONCLUSION

In this chapter we sought to distinguish between management and leadership, and to develop understandings related to the aspects of each that contribute to positive school cultures. More specifically, we focused attention on the importance of both management and leadership, suggesting that these concepts are often hard to distinguish in practice. As principals seek to intensify leadership, they must feel confident in their ability to perform both. We also contend that school cultures are shaped by the choices leaders make in a variety of arenas and with a variety of subgroups and members. In this way, we argue that culture is not monolithic nor is a process for leading cultural change easily outlined or described. Instead we suggest that cultural change is enhanced by intensifying leadership within the school. We next turn our attention to thinking more specifically about how leaders can diagnosis the culture of their schools and the ways in which professional community, organizational learning, and trust can inform those efforts.

ADDITIONAL READINGS AND
ACTIVITIES FOR GETTING STARTED

In this chapter we suggest readings that will extend your learning, as well as activities for reflection. The recommended readings challenge your thinking because they look at the problems of organizations (and schools) in fresh and unconventional ways. The activities expand on the cases in the chapter and ask you to consider alternative outcomes.

Readings

Mitroff, I. (1998). *Smart thinking for crazy times.* San Francisco: Berrett-Koehler.

Mitroff always thinks a little more "out of the box" than most management writers. This book, though it might look like a management text, is really a primer on the critical questions that need to be asked as part of analyzing and changing an organizational system. A quick read, it focuses less on the leader and more on the complexity of problem solving. The first third of the book, which poses critical questions for analyzing system problems, is the best. Particularly important for school settings is the discussion of how to formulate problems and how to choose the right stakeholders.

Morgan, G. (1997). *Imaginization.* Thousand Oaks, CA: Sage.

Less a "normal book" than a collection of ideas and tools that you can use to help both yourself and those that you work with to see things differently, this book is invaluable. The materials in the book speak to the heart and ideas that are often "beyond words" but help to shake up a meeting or a discussion so that people can move beyond current positions. Use it to shake up your own ideas, or those of your school improvement team! And then go and read other books by Gareth Morgan.

Quinn, R. (1996). *Deep change: Discovering the leader within you.* San Francisco: Jossey-Bass.

Being a change manager means looking inward to the personal issues that are raised by change. This book presents some of the most critical ideas about personal change in the context of being responsible for changing an organization and the lives of others. Without this book, you may inadvertently become "part of the problem" in spite of your best efforts. What is the alternative to deep change on a personal level? Slow death. . . . Quinn argues persuasively that you cannot encourage others to make deep changes unless you are willing to make them yourself.

Activities

Beyond Metro High

The story of Metro High ends in a surprising way. Though efforts at Metro resulted in increased test scores on graduation exams and a decrease in dropout rates, these successes were not enough to prevent other more threatening challenges. Located at the core of an urban city, the neighborhood that had once supported Metro had been slowly replaced by office buildings and hospital complexes. Enrollment across the district was shrinking and the building was aging. A levy had failed. In the fall of 2007, district leadership determined that as a cost-cutting measure they would close several schools in June. Metro was one of them. At this writing, the faculty have either retired or been transferred to other schools within the system. One will be assigned to the district office as an assessment coordinator, and she hopes that she can continue the work she began at Metro.

1. What are the significant aspects of the "plot line" related to the progression of events in the case? (You might want to develop a chronology to represent the events as they unfolded.)

2. What aspects of the PCOLT, intensified leadership, and culture can you bring to understanding the events?

3. Why do you think that even in the face of steady improvement the district would choose to close Metro? What might the principal have done to better protect or defend the school from its eventual closing?

4. What relevance does this case have to your own experiences?

Reflection

Look back at Figure 1.1, which suggests several dimensions that need to be balanced. In what cells are the pressures on you the most serious? Where do you spend most of your time? Where are the areas of your leadership practice that require more balance? How do you think you might begin to develop balance in your practice? What would be the benefits to and results of your work?

Look back at Figure 2.4. On what leadership behaviors do you spend most of your time? On which management behaviors do you spend most of your time? What other people in your school engage in leadership and management behaviors such as those listed in the figure? Are there any that are underemphasized?

ANALYZING YOUR SCHOOL

Considering Cultural Leadership and Management

Reflect on the leadership and management tasks discussed in this chapter. In the table below note on which of the leadership and management behaviors you spend your time. Rank these as considerable attention (daily or at least weekly), some attention (monthly or quarterly), or minor attention (yearly or less).

Note those that you primarily attend to on your own as well as those in which others are involved. Where is the time in your school invested? What areas are currently underemphasized?

Cultural Management					
	Considerable Attention	Some Attention	Minor Attention	Individual	Team
Creative problem solving					
Working within the current paradigm					
Providing sustained support or aid for teachers and improvement initiatives					
Moving things and people into motion					
Creating an attitude of doing					
Providing for oversight and mutual accountability					
Cultural Leadership					
Discovering new possibilities and developing capacity to realize them					
Creating a new paradigm or vision					
Promoting inclusion and dignity for all					
Empowering staff, students, and stakeholders					
Changing the system					
Creating an attitude of serving					

3

Diagnosing Your School Culture

Understanding Where You Are

Knowing the stakeholders, the cultural arenas, and the contextual features that you must consider is just a start. You must also deepen your knowledge of your school before you can move forward to create a more dynamic and adaptable school culture.

In this chapter you will:

- learn about diagnosing the culture of your school;
- begin to set an agenda for change based on your diagnosis; and
- start to intensify leadership at your school by using diagnosis to find and develop your team players.

We argue that it is not possible to distribute or intensify leadership in your school without a basic understanding of your current conditions. In addition, without a clear diagnosis of your school's culture, you and your staff may not make the best choices about how to adapt to internal and external pressures. In other words, reaching agreement about how the culture needs to be changed is a first but critical step on the road to improving student learning. A brief example will suffice.

VALLEYFIELD HIGH SCHOOL'S "COMPREHENSIVE REFORM" EFFORT

Valleyfield is a rural community with many big-city ills. The local economy was based on a food-packing plant that lured low-skilled workers for several decades but relocated out of the state several years ago. Unemployment is high and prospects for economic revitalization seem weak. Few professionals (including teachers) live in Valleyfield anymore, and many of the lovely Victorian homes appear to be crumbling. School achievement is improving in the elementary schools, but remains low at Valleyfield High. Nevertheless, most teachers believe that they are doing their best under difficult circumstances.

Several years ago the state "diagnosed" the school as poor and low performing, and provided significant resources and technical assistance to promote improvement. Part of the arrangement was that the school was to implement a comprehensive reform program that came with staff development assistance. While there was some debate, the teachers (with Principal Ira Greene's approval) quickly settled on a well-known national program. On the surface, this seemed reasonable because the program had demonstrated effectiveness with at-risk students. Everyone in the school acknowledges, however, that the main reason was that it required less change in instructional and school organization than other alternatives. The English department has persisted in trying to offer seminar experiences, one of three main foci of the program, but a social studies teacher confided that "most teachers just relabeled their existing assignments as "projects" and "coaching."

The problem in Valleyfield was not that teachers were lazy (though a few were) but that the existing culture emphasized two core beliefs: that Valleyfield students would be doing well if they graduated from high school, and that teachers were doing the best that they could possibly do. There was little or no discussion about teaching and instruction, and Principal Greene focused on maintaining discipline and not disrupting an elaborate administrative system that supported department autonomy. The principal, who was well liked personally but more concerned about maintaining the system than changing it, did not foster conversations about the kind of changes that might be needed in order to move forward.

On the other hand, no one helped Principal Greene, whose heart was in the right place, to understand the need to diagnose the school's culture. In this chapter, we expand on the ideas in Chapter 2 by further exploring culture and the potential for management and leadership to change school culture. In this way, we hope to provide school leaders clear ideas and directions with which they may begin changing their school culture. We will return to the Valleyfield example later, to find out how diagnosing culture played a part in a transformation that occurred when the principal retired.

THE BASICS OF CULTURAL DIAGNOSIS

Our suggested approach draws on the work of numerous people who have written about organizational culture, but is most firmly rooted in the work of Edgar Schein (2004). In order to diagnose a school's culture, we need to examine the multiple levels at which culture is manifested in organizations (Hofstede, Neuijen, Ohayv, & Sanders, 1990; Pettigrew, 1990). Schein suggests that culture has three distinct parts: artifacts, espoused values, and underlying assumptions. You might consider these as organizational layers, starting with the most visible and moving toward a central core of taken-for-granted assumptions concerning "how we do things around here."

At one level, *cultural artifacts* are revealed by what that one sees, hears, and feels when entering an organization. Artifacts include the unique symbols, heroes, rites and rituals, myths, ceremonies, and sagas of an organization (Hofstede, 1991; Trice & Beyer, 1984). Artifacts of culture are easy to observe but more difficult to interpret (Schein, 2004). In schools, these may include the building itself (very tidy or cheerfully chaotic?), the ways students dress (uniforms or street clothes? expensive or hand-me-downs?), or observable rituals (pep assemblies every Friday? recitation of the pledge of allegiance in every classroom?). A school's artifacts are intended to communicate both to those inside the school and to visitors what the school believes itself to be. They are important, but people who are used to them may not see them for what they are: collective expressions of values and expected patterns of behavior.

Espoused values include what people can tell you about enduring beliefs or tendencies to prefer certain modes of conduct or states of affairs over another, and they are what most people look for to identify a culture (Rokeach, 1973). Values represent articulated "shoulds" and "oughts" of organizational culture. Like artifacts, they are often taken for granted, but even when they are not talked about they provide strong guidelines for how to act.

Consistent with the general organizational literature, most educational researchers treat shared values as a defining aspect of culture (Deal & Peterson, 1991; Hoy & Miskel, 1996). The conversations within a school often occur when someone has violated some values, creating a need to clarify what people want and how much variation they are willing to accept. A common area where this can be seen is around the content and format of staff meetings—how long they should last, who should talk first or last, and what topics are out of bounds.

According to many organizational experts, one must look deeper than values to find the essence of a culture. What people say should or ought to be is often inconsistent with their actual behavior because espoused values often suggest where we wish to be rather than where we currently find ourselves (Argyris & Schön, 1974). For example, when we speak with school leaders and teachers, they often claim that parents are important members of the school community. Yet, parents are rarely asked to play important roles in school leadership or governance, and are not expected to contribute to decisions related to curriculum or the day-to-day operation of the school. This is usually the case because professionals have had mixed experiences with interference or lack of responsiveness: "Our parents are too busy" or "Parents usually come in only when they want something for their own kids."

These "taken-for-granted" assumptions are often difficult to expose because organizational members are often unaware that they exist and that they are following them. For example, as a group, teachers may view teaching as an art or a skill, their colleagues as resources or rivals, and attending workshops as essential to improved practice or a waste of time. These collective assumptions are rarely discussed, but they influence both daily work and whether change is embraced or viewed with trepidation.

Underlying assumptions also influence the school culture by clouding (or illuminating) what and how we hear organizational messages. Teachers at a school with an underlying cultural assumption that students come to school with habits that impede their learning hear the words "We can to do better" as an unfair and misplaced accusation or as a threat to future job security. Yet, in a school with a culture that focuses on continual improvement and where there is a high sense of collective efficacy, the same words might be heard as encouragement or confirmation of a valued outcome. The words are the same; it is the underlying assumption about what they mean that makes all the difference.

FOUR CULTURAL ORIENTATIONS: WHERE DOES YOUR SCHOOL FIT?

The importance of underlying assumptions is described as falling into four basic types by Harrison and Stokes (1992):

- A *power orientation* values organizational strength, justice, and benevolence. It sees the school as the primary source of resources that create opportunities for children and rewards for staff, and outsiders as hostile or uninformed.
- A *role orientation* values order, dependability, rationality, and consistency. It assumes that people—teachers, students, and administrators—will do their best when they can count on everyone to work toward common goals in agreed-upon ways. Dependability may, on the other hand, become rigidity.
- An *achievement orientation* values work that engages the whole person, and assumes that it is best when students and teachers supervise themselves, work in teams, and have a sense of energy and urgency. At an extreme, this kind of school may create unremitting pressure and a sense of competition for both staff and students.
- A *support orientation* values people helping each other, communicating, collaborating, and caring for the school and its members. People trust that the school will take care of their individual needs whenever possible. In a worst case, short-term caring may drive out serious attention to long-range learning and development needs.

In summary, a school's culture is like an iceberg, where most of what is important is submerged (Figure 3.1). What you see is not always what is important, and it is the less visible parts of a school's culture that often throw a monkey wrench into change efforts. Most of a school's culture lies below what can be easily seen, and the members of most schools talk more often about artifacts (How can we keep the halls cleaner? Should we have a pop machine available all day? What rules should we have for student behavior in the cafeteria?). Your job, as a diagnostician, is to come to a better understanding of both espoused values and basic underlying assumptions.

Figure 3.1   Layers of School Culture

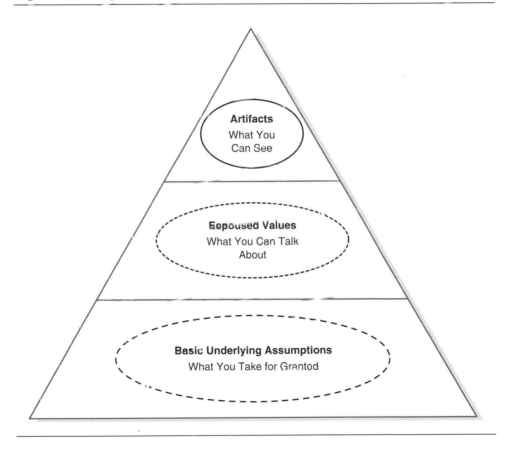

When school leaders embark on the work of cultural change, it is impor-tant that they understand the ways in which all three levels operate in their schools. Doing so allows you to answer key culture questions, including:

- What do we see when we walk into the building that demonstrates who we are? (Surface artifacts)
- What do we think is important? How is this visible in our school? (Deeper artifacts)

- How do we express what we value? When and where do we talk about it? (Espoused values)
- Where might we like to be in a year? Three years? Five years? Ten years? (Espoused values)
- How do tensions in our school and divergence between what we want and what we can accomplish reveal our culture? (Basic underlying assumptions)

DIAGNOSING YOUR SCHOOL CULTURE

There are many approaches to diagnosing culture. To get at the deepest level of basic underlying assumptions may require a trained outsider, who spends quite a bit of time in the setting, and talks to all or most of the people who represent different stakeholder groups (Schein, 1993). Many corporations hire consultants to do this, and most publications about organizational diagnosis are written with a consultant in mind. However, an intensive use of highly paid external partners is typically beyond the means of a public school. This chapter is, therefore, intended to be deliberately practical, focusing on what principals and their team members can do to get this process started. In general, we recommend that principals think about cultural diagnosis as a three-stage process, shown in Figure 3.2.

The figure looks simple, but its point is that cultural diagnosis is a repeated cyclical process of gathering, analyzing, and reflecting on information that involves multiple passes, but usually with a different group of people, and a deepening understanding.

- During the first "wet" phase, you probably will feel most comfortable working by yourself or with a few close colleagues whom you trust. Cultural diagnosis can be tricky, and you want to make sure that you have done your best to understand your school on your own *and* that you are personally prepared to participate in a changed culture in which your work, as well that of others, will be altered.
- Once you have conducted a preliminary diagnosis, you will need to enter a "wash" phase that includes a sizeable team—possibly even the whole school staff if it is small. We call it *wash* because it is during this phase that you may begin to uncover issues and feelings that need to be dealt with. It is important at this stage to rely on volunteers, because the work is hard and it is important to be transparent. Who should be included is a decision that we discuss in more detail below, but you should remember that the purpose is to uncover and even begin to get rid of what can hold you back.
- On a later pass, you will need to include other stakeholders, particularly key people outside the school who need to be involved if the culture is really to change. This is the "rinse" phase in the sense that whatever you have discovered during your broader team "washing" activities will need to be acknowledged and dealt with if you are to

Figure 3.2   Cultural Diagnosis: Wet, Wash, Rinse, Repeat

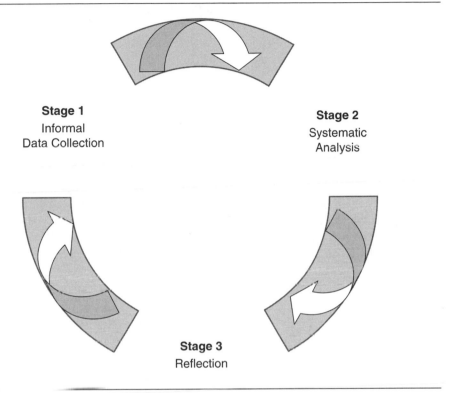

Stage 1
Informal
Data Collection

Stage 2
Systematic
Analysis

Stage 3
Reflection

intensify leadership for school improvement. How to make this process one that is positive but cathartic also will be discussed below.

Wet: Getting Ready for Deep Change

Robert Quinn (1996) has argued that you cannot lead change in your organization until you prepare to transform yourself. We agree, and have found that many of the educators we have worked with look at faltering change efforts in their own organization and understand that one of the reasons is that they did not prepare themselves to model the change that they expect of others. The temptation is to get going right away—find a good survey, gather the data, and forge ahead. This can be a mistake, because if you have not prepared yourself you may be tempted to become personally detached from the process and see culture change as something that other people need to do.

Becoming fully wet does not require engaging in intensive therapeutic self-inquiry, nor postponing needed changes while you root out all of your peccadilloes as a leader. It does, however, require that you begin to review what *you* take for granted and would rather not change. We contend that you will be better prepared to help others change (and in the process intensify leadership) if you are thoughtful about assessing your own assumptions about your school's culture.

In fact, we think that this first phase can be quite straightforward except under two conditions. The first is that you are a new administrator in a school that you are unfamiliar with; in this instance you will need early allies to help you understand unstated or undiscussed responses and behavior. The second is if you have been in your position for a rather long time. This usually means that your preferences and assumptions are so intertwined with the existing culture that it may be difficult for you to see the part that you play in maintaining the very behaviors that you would like to change.

VALLEYFIELD'S PRINCIPAL AND STUDENT BEHAVIOR

Principal Ira Greene, an African American, saw one of his primary responsibilities as being responsive to the needs of the largely white and very experienced staff. Many of the older teachers complained about students' public behavior. Their complaints never referred directly to the changed racial composition of the school, but there were frequent discussions about students who had weak disciplinary examples in the home and differences in cultural expectations. The principal responded over the years by instituting a system that "corralled" students in the auditorium as the buses arrived in the morning (which kept them out of the halls) and by spending much of his time roaming the building during passing periods to reprimand loud adolescent behavior. The in-school suspension room was filled every day with bored students doing little work.

A newly appointed associate superintendent who was asked to look at the implementation of the school's comprehensive reform was shocked by the description of the students as rowdy and badly behaved; students were, in fact, polite and generally quiet in the halls and cafeteria, even compared to rather affluent suburban schools that she had recently worked in. Race relations between the Hispanic and African American students in both the halls and cafeteria appeared to be respectful and friendly. When she reported her observation about the disjuncture between teacher complaints and actual student behavior, the principal pointed to his rules as "working" to contain unruly adolescents.

We argue that Ira Greene was so deeply embedded in the school's culture, in which student behavior was blamed for their low performance, that he could not see the that most students were engaged with the school and could have easily been motivated to work harder with a more positive disciplinary culture. He was caught in a system that combined a strong *role orientation* (with its emphasis on routines and order) and a *support orientation* (which was caring, but in this case largely focused on the faculty's needs).

So what are some simple things that you can do to prepare yourself for a mind-opening diagnosis?

- *A quick "cultural pulse taking."* On your own, think about the school's culture and answer the following questions in writing (we are sure that you have already thought about the answers).

    ○ What is the level of trust and/or conflict among teachers?
    ○ Are instructional and curricular decisions openly discussed?
    ○ Do members value each other and do they work together well?
    ○ Are communication structures open and honest?
    ○ Is learning something in which everyone is engaged or is it what the kids do?
    ○ Who makes most of the decisions in the school? What happens if people don't agree with a decision that has been made?
    ○ Do people seem to like working here? Who, if anyone, seems to be dissatisfied?

Knowing the answers to these culture questions allows you to diagnose where the strengths and weakness of your school organization lie. These and similar questions will help get you started thinking about your building as a place in which people work together to promote student learning.

- *A "walkabout."* On your own (or, even better, with another person who knows the school well), spend a day or so simply observing your school. Try not to get distracted with the usual array of "things that need to be done right now" because if you do, you will be unable to be a detached observer. In particular, look for artifacts, especially the following:

    ○ Observe what happens as the school comes to life in the morning. What do people see when they first come into the building? What evidence do they have that this is a place where adults and students are learning? What do people look like when they come in the morning? Are they cheerful and happy, or grumpy?

    ○ Watch hard to see how adults interact in public spaces. What do they talk about when they have quick interactions during the day? How do adults treat students in the hallways? How do the various other people in the school, from counselors to cafeteria staff, work with each other and students?

    ○ Follow a "typical" student (neither a top performer nor a troublemaker) for half a day and try to see the school through his or her eyes. How do students react to each other? How about to their exchanges with adults?

    ○ Look for physical evidence of the school's cultural norms and values. What physical evidence would an outsider see about the value placed on student learning? Is there any evidence, in the halls or other public places, that suggests that student work is valued?

You may, of course, also take your walkabout into classrooms, in which case you should look for evidence of student engagement, respectful interaction, and the physical evidence in classrooms that teachers are teaching and students are learning. The point of these classroom visits is not to evaluate individual teachers, but to look for evidence that allows you to assess the culture of the school. It may also be useful to attend teacher meetings wearing your observer's hat, to think carefully about what is happening that suggest that teachers are taking on leadership for student learning and school improvement. If you attend meetings and observe classrooms, you should make it clear that you are there just to catch up on what's going on, and not in a supervisory role.

- *A formal inventory with notes.* Go back to the questions we have listed and write about what you have observed. Administer a survey (see chapter resources) to teachers, students, parents, and others.

When you have gathered some "data" that you didn't have before, you need to analyze it:

- *Summarize what you think you know.* Put your observations into the three "big bins" that we have suggested are the most important elements of a school's culture: professional community, organizational learning, and trust. What surprised you, if anything? What did you see that evoked emotional responses in you?

The final part of getting wet is to spend time reflecting on what you learned. Since this phase is about challenging yourself, you should:

- *Assess yourself as a cultural leader.* Seriously consider what you have done to foster improvements in the organizational culture. Where have you put your energy? What might you have ignored or paid insufficient attention to? Write a paragraph about yourself as a cultural leader today, and write another describing the ways in which you would like to change.

This work brings you to the end of the first diagnosis cycle. You have gathered data on your school's culture, analyzed it, and reflected on its meaning for you as a cultural leader. You are ready, as Robert Quinn puts it, to "walk naked into the land of uncertainty" (Quinn, 1996, p. 3) as you involve others in this work. Before turning to what happens in the wash cycle, let's look at the experiences of a principal who really understood the meaning of "getting wet" in her school's culture.

USING PERSONAL INSIGHT TO SET AN AGENDA FOR CHANGE

Cheryl Lowe came to the principalship at Hill Elementary with a decade of experience. When she interviewed, the team made it clear that they were looking for a leader that would "fit" with a staff focused on change and continuous improvement. She assured them that she could support their vision. In preparing for the fall, she spent her summer studying the school's achievement data, curriculum resources, and improvement plan. She saw that a lot of work was being carried out—in the past year alone; six new programs had been adopted. But it was hard to understand how all the pieces fit together and test scores were bottoming out after a few years of improvement. She began to suspect that the school needed to be involved with fewer, more focused initiatives. This insight troubled her. After all, she had agreed to support the efforts that teachers had invested in.

As August grew closer, Lowe carefully considered the first faculty meeting. How much of her analysis should she share? What would happen if the faculty thought she was overstepping? She decided all she could do was dive in: "It was better than lying to them. . . ." As the faculty and staff assembled, she warmly greeted each one. After breakfast, she started out with the story of her excitement of accepting the position and how she began her summer work. Without offering much detail, she shared the results of her analysis and her concerns that they would think she had betrayed them. She finished by saying, "I took this job because I was convinced that you all were good people. People I wanted to work with. But I think you've all been working at way too much. I'm hoping that this year we can agree to do less but make more happen." Then she sat down. Within minutes, a voice from the back yelled out, "That makes more sense than anything I've heard in a long while."

Cheryl Lowe's story is heartening; she paid attention to the *meaning* of the initial interview, and didn't forget what people were really trying to tell her once she got the job. She spent a lot of time looking at artifacts, and thinking deeply about their meaning. More important, she was willing to reveal herself and her own doubts to a faculty that barely knew her, trusting that honesty, openness, and the various charts that she had assembled were a better introduction than waiting for a behind-the-scenes approach to a serious challenge that faces many faculty: What are we willing to give up in order to move forward? She didn't present them with a solution, but with evidence that there was further need for diagnosis.

Wash: Creating Broader Energy for Diagnosis

Principals and administrative teams should recognize before they start that it is not possible for an *effective* cultural diagnosis to be carried out by a small number of people, and that they cannot mandate change without changing themselves. Nothing is wrong with improving your own understanding of your school's culture—like Cheryl Lowe, you need to start there—but change that requires shifts in a school's culture requires that others develop and share the same understanding.

Why is this need for intensified leadership in diagnosis so central? The answer lies in the basic fact that culture is learned and, like most things that you "just know," you take it for granted. New staff members in a school generally are less likely to learn the culture by participating in formal "new teacher" programs than through informal conversations where the stories of "how we do things around here" are shared. They quickly learn the rituals of the place, how the buses line up, how students are expected to walk in the hallways, and who may speak and when they may do so.

These regularities of school life may be annoying at times, but they are also a source of comfort because people like to wake up knowing that most of what happens to them can be anticipated. When a culture is well learned, it is extremely difficult to change unless most people want it to. Unless you are an exceptionally charismatic leader, your chances of persuading teachers, parents, and students to upend their usual behaviors and expectations are very, very limited.

VALLEYFIELD'S CULTURE RECONSIDERED

When Ira Greene retired, Norma Shale, who had been an assistant principal for five years, succeeded him. Norma had already conducted her own wet cycle in preparation for applying for the principal's position, and, like Hill Elementary's Principal Lowe, she saw herself as ready to move. Her initial reaction was to make a few visible changes that would demonstrate that she was ready to move: She eliminated the auditorium "corral" before the start of the school day, replacing it with an opportunity for early-arriving students to either mingle with others in the cafeteria or to meet with teachers, and set aside a room for teacher professional development and meetings, stocking it with a small library of reading material.

She was aided in the transition by the district's "request" that the school discontinue their comprehensive reform program and implement an alternative model that required the formal participation of teacher leaders. Using the support provided by the program's developer, Principal Shale was able to quickly identify a group of teachers who were eager to change and who understood that the old culture had to be challenged.

Principal Shale didn't have this book to help her, but she did, informally, engage in several of the diagnostic strategies that we suggest for the next phase: eliminating some artifacts and replacing them with others, finding a group of teachers who were perceived as leaders by their peers and who were ready to challenge the status quo, and working with them to think about and resolve issues facing the culture change that was required in the school. Her work was, implicitly, guided by her reliance on the PCOLT foundation, relying on existing professional communities (which existed in some departments), and building new ones (the teacher team required by the developer of the new comprehensive reform program); taking advantage of the learning that could come by taking the core concepts of the program seriously; and drawing on her own personal warmth and goodwill to reinforce the trust that teachers had generally placed in her as the assistant principal.

Norma Shale did not engage in a formal wash phase. Though she and her team continued to think about the school's culture, they didn't gather and analyze data in a systematic fashion. What could she have done if she wanted to be more systematic, given that she did not have access to an outside consultant? We suggest three approaches that any principal can easily incorporate to set the stage for a firmer understanding of the school's culture, each of which could be useful by itself or in combination: appreciative inquiry, force-field analysis, and survey feedback. We will briefly describe each of these, as well as provide more information in the resources section of this chapter.

Appreciative Inquiry (AI)

As an action for surfacing organizational culture, AI is the most recently introduced strategy of the three, but it is also one that is uniquely adapted for working within strong culture organizations, like Valleyfield High School, in which there are many layers of attachment and emotion that pervade teacher's attachment to the "way we do things around here." Many schools are like Valleyfield, with attachments to their culture that are bluntly described as:

> Organizational members become committed to a pattern of behavior. . . . In a desire to avoid embarrassment and threat, few if any challenges are made to the wisdom and viability of these behaviors. They persist even when rapid and fundamental shifts in the competitive environment render these patterns of behavior obsolete. (Beer & Spector, 1993, p. 642)

The paradox of AI diagnosis is that understanding what needs to change sometimes works best by first increasing the group's understanding of what works well. Why is this the case? Largely because diagnosis, even if accurate, never will lead to change unless the members of the organization believe, in their hearts, that the data are valid and true. In addition, the basic tools of AI can be presented to schools as a variation on action research (Cooperider & Srivasta, 1997), a concept that many educators are at least familiar with even if they have never been involved in it. This is the premise underlying our recommendation that many schools begin their wash with AI. What does AI consist of? One of the prominent developers describes it this way:

> AI seeks, fundamentally, to build a constructive union between what people talk about as past and present capacities including:

achievements, assets, unexplored potentials, innovations, trengths, elevated thoughts, opportunities, benchmarks, high point moments, lived values, traditions, strategic competencies, stories, expressions of wisdom, insights into the deeper corporate spirit or soul—and visions of valued and possible futures. (Cooperider & Whitney, 2004, p. 3)

AI is divided into four phases, which are illustrated in Figure 3.3. The first step of the process is indicated by choosing a question that is really important to the school. Cooperider and Whitney call this the "affirmative topic choice." The question needs to be manageable and of concern to most people. The choice should be posed in a positive light. In the case of Valleyfield High School, for example, "How can we provide consistent support for student learning?" is a more desirable affirmative topic choice than "How can we improve low test scores?"

Carrying Out Appreciative Inquiry Phases

AI, unlike the two other diagnostic approaches we will discuss, is a rather lengthy process. In general, because a lot of new data must be collected and analyzed, you should be prepared for this work to take up to a full school year. Remember the underlying assumption: to build the culture and intensify leadership as part of diagnosis means that shortening the number of people involved and doing the job more quickly will limit learning and the possibility of "softening" the existing culture. If you are the impatient type, or the pressures on the school for change are enormous, AI may not be the place to begin. On the other hand, it can easily be carried out as part of the culture-building process when some consensus about critical areas of action has been agreed upon. As we describe the four phases, you will see that you cannot carry a full AI process out in one or two meetings!

The *discovery phase* involves a broad effort (in this case, by the core team) to find out what people think they are already doing well around this topic. This phase should be quite exhaustive, and allow as many people as possible to contribute. The best way of getting this information is to get every member of your team to "interview" several other faculty members—not just the "go-getters" who are ready to move, but also those that are "stuck" and likely to oppose major changes. The point is to allow people the chance to articulate at a personal level what they are proud of and to give specific examples that point to their success. A formal summary and discussion should be made to ensure that the list of positives—and examples of what has worked well—is complete and fully representative of the school. This is a time to consider involving staff members other than faculty—you may be surprised at what the social worker or the school secretary may say about how they see themselves contributing.

The *dream phase* involves serious consideration of what the "ideal school" would be like if it were doing this well. It is important in this phase not to limit your team's imagination to what they think that your

Figure 3.3 The AI Process

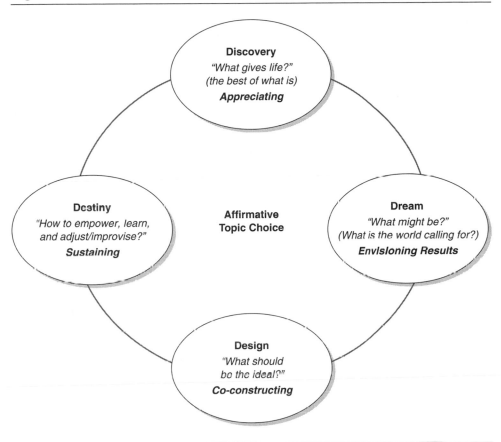

SOURCE: Adapted from D. Cooperider & D. Whitney. (2004). *A positive revolution in change: Appreciative inquiry* (p. 30). Retrieved August 16, 2007, from http://appreciativeinquiry.case .edu/uploads/whatisai.pdf

school could do; the goal is to genuinely dream. The dream phase should not be too brief, because if you try to do this in one or two meetings, people will not be encouraged to truly think "outside the box." One good way of stimulating conversations about the dream is to think of analogies and tie these back to the core questions: What if schools were like healthy, happy families? What if schools were like jet planes? What if schools were like organic farms? The analogies are unlimited, and you can choose the ones that are most helpful, but they allow people to think about other kinds of organizing that could connect with a "dream."

The *design phase* involves thinking about alternatives that could map the dream onto the existing organization. While some advocate doing this in a large group format, we think that, unless your school is very small and quite cohesive, it is better to work first within your team. In this way, you may avoid the cynicism and negativity that characterizes some school staffs. One outcome might be a set of visionary propositions about what could change in the school to take steps toward the dream that emerged in the previous phase. Note that at this point there is no need to edit or prioritize, except possibly to eliminate those that everyone agrees are either undesirable or totally unachievable.

The *destiny phase* is often best left to the rinse cycle because it involves broad sharing—not of a vision, but of the design propositions—and enlarging involvement of more faculty (and others) in working on fleshing them out, making them a reality, and monitoring progress toward the goal of the central, affirmative topic choice.

Force-Field Analysis

Another useful diagnostic tool is force-field analysis, a technique that was first proposed by Kurt Lewin in the 1940s, which has long been a staple of change agents in the business sector. Force-field techniques are generally most appropriate when the school has already reached some consensus about a need for change—if that does not exist, we suggest that you start with AI. We advocate force-field analysis because we believe that it generates clear guides to action, albeit less visionary in focus than AI.

The process of conducting a force-field analysis is not complex and works well with small or large groups. In other words, it can be used with a whole school, but you definitely will want to try it out first with your team in the wash. Remember that the facilitator must be a neutral figure and cannot inject opinions into the discussion, so you may want to recruit someone else (a faculty member from a local university or a sympathetic administrator from the district or another school) for the role. This technique is among the best we know of to address the challenge of apathy because it can produce new insights and knowledge in a very short amount of time. In some cases, a force-field analysis can be used to create energy, which can then be pushed back into the longer process of carrying out AI. The order and combination of diagnostic processes is up to you and your core team, once everyone understands what they entail.

What Is Force-Field Analysis?

A force-field analysis is based on the assumption that the people who work in schools are like the proverbial blind men and an elephant. Each one feels different parts of the beast (in this case, the way in which the school is organized to promote student learning), but they don't see the same things. The goal of a force-field analysis is to put the insights from those who have grabbed hold of the elephant's tail with those who are patting its ears. Only when we understand the totality of the elephant—the systemic character of the school—can we prepare for change.

Force-field analysis encourages your staff to think about their school as a system—an elephant rather than the discrete anatomical parts of an elephant—and how those parts work for and against the status quo. In a period when schools are being asked to engage not only in improving instruction, but also in becoming more responsive to parents and state standards, the force-field process is helpful in getting staff members to think about the "big picture." As Beer and Spector note, not only is the school part of a larger system, but as we have noted above, it also has many subsystems. Again, an effective force-field analysis can reveal which of those subsystems are most important (Beer & Spector, 1993).

Like AI, it also looks at the positive. Unlike AI, it requires staff to also look at weaknesses. Its purpose is to help teams to look at the issues that they face as a function of these two sets of offsetting factors. The essence of a force field analysis in Valleyfield is conveyed visually in Figure 3.4.

Force-field techniques can be used to frame existing problems or to anticipate factors that might emerge in the process of change. When it is used to define a problem more clearly, force-field analysis is helpful in pushing groups to pinpoint underlying issues in the school, such as morale, communication, effectiveness, and work climate. Force-field analysis also helps keep team members grounded in reality when they start planning a change by making them systematically anticipate what kind of resistance they could meet. Conducting a force-field analysis can build consensus by making it easy to discuss people's objections and then examining how to address these concerns.

How to Conduct a Force-Field Analysis

Conducting a force-field analysis is relatively straightforward. Here we cover the basics so that you can see how simple it is (adapted from a public access Web site for health care professionals: http://www.qaproject .org/methods/resforcefield.html). More details and suggestions are given in the resources section at the end of this chapter.

Step 1. State the problem or desired state and make sure that all team members understand it. You can construct the statement in terms of factors working for and against a desired state (if you all agree on an ideal) or in terms of factors working for and against the status quo or problem state (if you agree that a problem exists but not on the ideal state). Make sure that there is consensus and understanding at this point or eventually you will have to start over!

Step 2. Brainstorm the positive and negative forces. You don't have to be definitive the first time around. You can add forces later in the discussion.

Figure 3.4   Sample Problem Statement: Need Better Use of All Staff to Support Student Learning

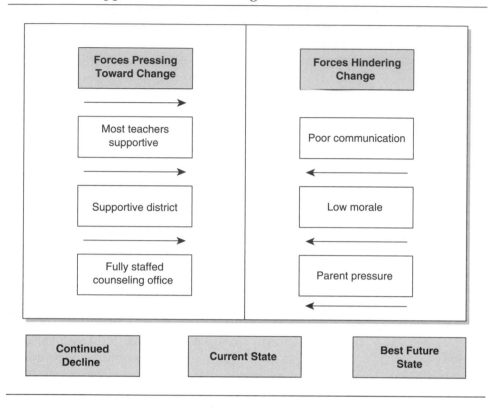

Step 3. Review and clarify each force or factor. What is behind each factor? What works to balance the situation? This discussion is very important, and may allow you to add or change the factors that you have generated in Step 2.

Step 4. When you can reach consensus on a reasonable list of important factors, determine the strength of hindering forces (high, medium, low) in achieving the desired state or from improving the problem state. When the force-field technique is used for problem analysis, the forces with the biggest impact should be tested as likely causes. If the force-field analysis is used to develop solutions, those factors with the biggest impact may become the focus of plans to reduce resistance to change.

Step 5. Develop an action plan to address the largest hindering forces.

Where you start with a force-field analysis depends to a great extent on your initial analysis of the existing energy and interest within the student support staff members. If they are raring to go, you should start by examining the state of the school's readiness to implement new programs. If teachers and support staff members are not committed to change, you need to examine the conditions within the system itself, looking for barriers to change.

Alternative Ways to Reveal Barriers

Remember that the purpose of force-field analysis is to (1) analyze the present situation and (2) determine some of the initial changes that may be required to smooth the path toward change. Some of the forces that come up will be cultural; others may be political or relate to resource constraints. In general, we argue, the cultural barriers are the ones that schools are most able to deal with themselves because they involve looking primarily at relationships and beliefs. However, in many cases a force-field analysis may point to noncultural aspects of the school's situation that demand immediate and prior action. Remember: culture is not easy to change, and if you can get rid of a simple irritant without having to change people's hearts and minds, by all means do so—remembering the example of Valleyfield's new principal, Norma Shale, who made several key changes in how students were treated (modeling her respect for and belief in them) before she began to introduce other serious questions.

Finally, your school may be part of a larger, districtwide improvement initiative that uses other tools, such as strategic planning SWOT (strengths-weaknesses-opportunities-threats) analysis, which is often based on existing survey instruments, and other more formal data gathering methods. Many Web sites provide a quick and free introduction on how to conduct a SWOT analysis (a recent Google search produced almost 400,000), though we have some favorites that seem more applicable to a school setting. The most important caution that we offer is that, no matter how tempting it is, don't conduct a SWOT or a force-field analysis by yourself and present it to your staff. Its value, like that of the force-field analysis, is to "unfreeze" people's thinking about where they are and where they need to go.

Survey Feedback

If your staff is already attuned to and comfortable with numbers and data, we recommend that you consider using surveys as part of your diagnosis. There are, however, two drawbacks to consider.

First, unless you are in a large district with the capacity to help you administer and score the surveys, or are willing to use the free services provided by some professional associations (see the resources section at the end of this chapter), you will need to hire someone to do the number crunching. Several advantages outweigh the potential cost, however. First, "numbers don't lie," and if everyone answers the survey, the results will have to be taken seriously. Second, survey data can usually be used to generate discussion that lasts; the results provide a baseline for determining if things are improving, and if you use an established survey you may have the results from other schools with which to compare yourself.

Second, finding a path through the thicket of available instruments is no simple matter. There is no list of good and easily available surveys that can tap school climate and culture. Conducting a survey may be the answer under only two circumstances: Do you have someone who has the time and energy to find the "right" survey for you, and do you (or your team) want to spend time reviewing candidates for a survey in your school? In general, we recommend that unless you can find support from your district or another source, or you have a friend in a local university or support agency that is willing to work with you during the process of getting the data and stimulating conversation, that you might wish to choose a method over which you have more personal control.

Rinse: Bringing Others Into the Diagnosis

If you are in a large school, we assume that you will be carrying out the wash phase primarily with a smaller group. We hope that you have included a variety of people in your team, from go-getters to "if it's not broke, don't fix it" types. However, even if your team has a broad cross section of people on it, successful change requires support from the larger group, and also from key groups like parents. If you are in a secondary school, it is also useful to have students on board as well—not only because they have good ideas, but also because they can get the best of plans off track if they don't see their interests reflected!

As you embark on this stage, it is important to remember that a great deal of evidence supports the contention that a small group can easily be given the task of carrying out a preliminary diagnosis, but persuading others that the work is true and useful requires that they participate in this final stage in some meaningful way. You cannot mandate culture change, no matter how sensible—as we have said before, it must come from the heart.

There are several ways to do this, and some that you should definitely avoid. But all of the approaches that we suggest fall into the category of an *interactive clinical* (Lundberg, 2000) approach that gives everyone a sense that they are participating in an open airing of ideas. The best way to think about this phase is as "embedded staff development," because you are focusing on creating shared meanings around the important values and goals of the school. Among the things you can do are:

1. *Minimize data collection; focus on analysis and reflection in a group setting.* This is a particularly useful approach if you anticipate that most people will be open to your diagnostic results. You might, for example, present them at a fall back-to-school day, and ask the larger group for embellishment, amendments, and elaborations. This is useful no matter what diagnostic tool you have used in the wash phase, because there is always room for more analytic and reflective work. If you don't have a half-day to devote to this activity, you can do an initial presentation and brainstorming, and use your team to lead further discussions in department or team meetings at a later time.

2. *Collect more data, using other stakeholders as informants*. If you have conducted a preliminary force-field analysis, for example, you might want to present the results but ask stakeholders to expand on the various forces pressing toward and against your desired ends. If your school has a culture in which people are reluctant to talk about things that aren't going well, this can be very freeing, and it can be an important first step toward a more open, risk-taking environment. Here is your opportunity to involve those traditionally forgotten or ignored in culture change efforts—parents, community members, and students. As we noted above, they provide useful lenses with which to view the school and fresh insights into how new ideas might be received or resisted.

3. *Plunge further into rinsing through the data*. At this point, many educational professionals are tired of being asked to become data analysts. However, we think that data can become an asset rather than a burden by dividing work into meaningful but layered units. The point of data analysis is to develop a deeper understanding about how the school has operated in the past (knowledge of what was) and with an eye toward the future (knowledge of what can be).

4. *Surface dreams (hopes) and concerns (fears) about change within the larger group*. New ideas and opportunities can bring a person to life— you don't know what's going to happen or where things might go. The sense of possibility can be exciting and can encourage many to set aside other projects and goals for the chance to participate in a new, exciting venture. However, for those who have lived through the disappointment of prior educational change efforts, a enthusiasm may be tempered by their memories of how many times plans haven't worked out. Furthermore, the political realities of schools suggest that those with the most to lose—folks who currently enjoy the way things are or believe that a change may come at the cost of their power and authority—may actively resist an examination of the school's culture.

As part of the rinse cycle, it is important to surface the emotions that change evokes. You may do this by any one of the data collection tools we discussed in the wash phase of this chapter—a force-field analysis done by the larger group may surface pockets of cynicism and doubt as well as reserves of promise and potential. The best-case scenario suggests that your effort goes forward with little resistance and great immediate success. The worst-case scenario suggests that you are met with early and ongoing opposition and defiant challenge. Trust your sense of the level of readiness within your school. Resistance suggests you may need to spend more time in the wet and wash cycles of diagnosis; however, early acceptance doesn't mean you should sprint through those phases. Remember, in the end the rinse phase will be only as successful as the stakeholder participants' perception of you and your team as committed, but open and ready for personal change and challenge.

Repeat

As this chapter has indicated, cultural diagnosis is both critical and time consuming. It is not, however, a onetime event. Schools are dynamic places, and a new culture becomes embedded, generating new artifacts, values, and underlying assumptions. People retire or move and new people replace them. What worked five years ago to energize and keep a school lively may not work, especially if the culture has shifted and you have not attended to it. In the next chapter, we will revisit a key example of how an effective leader can make serious mistakes if cultural diagnosis doesn't become part of the routines of the school.

DIAGNOSIS AND INTENSIFIED LEADERSHIP FOR CULTURAL CHANGE

When times are good, members are in harmony and balance, progress toward student learning and achievement goals is evident, and school cultures are considered excellent. However, when one of these areas falls out of balance, rapid deterioration can occur. When trust is eroded and values and norms are unclear, or when learning is stifled, school cultures suffer. School leaders in today's challenging educational environment must work to establish strong positive cultures. Diagnosing your school's culture is not just a step that prepares you for changing and improving your school—it is part of the work. Effective diagnostic processes are intimately tied to the development of PCOLT—professional community, organizational learning, and trust.

Diagnosis and Professional Community

Diagnosis, when carried out in a full wet-wash-rinse cycle, involves building professional community inside the school. First, you must consider, like the leaders in the cases discussed in this chapter, your own relationship to others in the building, and you must openly model thoughtful leadership. In doing so, you open up the rest of the faculty to the principles of professional community: focusing on values and norms that you hold in common (What is important to us?), reflective discussion (How can we embody what we value in our work?), shared practice (What is hard for us to do? Can we help each other?), and collective responsibility (we all own the effectiveness of this school). Almost by definition, when the members of your school begin to feel the sense of communal energy that comes from participating in diagnostic work, they will be drawn to taking more initiative to become leaders on their own.

Diagnosis and Organizational Learning

The diagnostic process involves collecting and analyzing data. When people participate in this activity, they are, by definition, learning together.

When they are involved in interpretation and analysis—even through a straightforward force-field activity—they become knowledge generators and users. To the degree that others are involved, particularly in the wash and rinse phases, in turning data and information into shared knowledge, your school will be well on its way to becoming a learning organization. You will be developing the "habits of mind" that have been forcefully spelled out by Peter Senge (2002), who has popularized the belief that all vital organizations are engaged in collective learning.

Diagnosis and Trust

Diagnosis means that you and others are willing to look at the issues that are embedded in any school setting. The point of becoming vulnerable is to build trust and drive out fear that being honest will result in social or professional "punishment." The most important part of an effective diagnosis is that people in your school will become willing to look at both the good and the bad, to attribute it to systems and not to individuals, and to realize that taking the risk to achieve a balanced and realistic perspective will not mean that individuals or the school suffers. Of course, a minimal level of trust is required in order to start an effective diagnosis, but the process of sharing and interpreting information in a neutral fashion is also a trust-building activity. When people trust, they will be more likely to step forward and volunteer to do more—even if more is initially limited to monitoring the halls, as in the case of Valleyfield High School.

You probably understand less about your school's culture than you think you do. You are part of it. Arriving at a better personal understanding of your school is, therefore, one major reason to diagnose. But there are other reasons to assess your culture before engaging in a major improvement effort. It gets people ready to move, helps to surface new leaders who are willing to be part of a change effort, and builds the capacity and belief of both educational professionals and parents that future actions will be built on a firm foundation. Most important, diagnosis is part of building culture, but it is also a key element of initiating change.

Diagnosis and Intensified Leadership

It is not possible to distribute or intensify leadership in your school without understanding your current culture. The process of diagnosis allows you, with the assistance of others, to set the stage to make the best choices that can be made to support a culture that puts teaching and learning at the center. Though you may begin the diagnosis process alone, the addition of teachers (and others) in the process, highlights their ability to meaningfully contribute to school change efforts. As members see themselves as an active part of understanding the school, they also begin to see themselves as capable of taking on an active role in making change.

ADDITIONAL CULTURE SURVEY RESOURCES AND ACTIVITIES

Major Indicators of a Healthy School Culture

A seventeen-item culture inventory developed at the University of Kentucky looks at three aspects of culture, as identified by Wagner and Madsen-Copas (2002): Collaboration, collegiality, and sense of efficacy. This tool can provide a quick test of the issues in your school, and is available at http://www.schoolculture.net/indicate.html (in order to get the survey instrument, you need to order a CD that is available from the Web site).

School Quality and Effectiveness

Some instruments focus on a single dimension of a school's culture, such as trust, but have different instruments for different kinds of respondents, such as administrators, teachers, parents, and students, such as Megan Tschannen-Moran's scale available at http://mxtsch.people .wm.edu/research_tools.php.

Additional surveys from Tschannen-Moran include an extensive inventory of more than 250 items that is based on school effectiveness research and is available from the National Education Association (http://www.nea.org/schoolquality/).

Student Surveys

School culture/climate surveys are designed for administration to students (see, for example, the online surveys available from Learning Point Associates at http://www.goal.learningpt.org/winss/scs/). While that may be useful at some point in your cultural journey, it is probably not the place to start.

Other excellent surveys have a singular focus on the school's focus on creating a good learning environment for students. WestEd's Healthy Kids School Climate Survey, available at http://www.wested.org/chks/ pdf/scs_flyer_04.pdf, offers one such tool; however, it does not provide information on other groups (e.g., staff, parents, administration) present within the school community.

Research and Evaluation

Some good surveys that were developed for research and evaluation purposes and are being spun off into distinct organizations that support administration and interpretation are available at www.schoolclimatesur vey.com/html/aboutus.htm.

Force-Field and SWOT Analysis

Should you wish more detailed directions for completing a force-field or SWOT analysis, several Web sites offer good directions and free worksheets to help guide the process:

http://www.mindtools.com/pages/article/newTED_06.htm

http://www.mycoted.com/Force-Field_Analysis/

http://www.skymark.com/resources/tools/force_field_diagram.asp

http://www.quickmba.com/strategy/swot/

http://www.mindtools.com/pages/article/newTMC_05.htm

An Additional Reading

Hord, S., & Sommers, W. (2008). *Leading professional learning communities: Voices from research and practice.* Thousand Oaks, CA: Corwin Press.

Hord has been a longtime thinker and seminal contributor to our understanding of how professional learning communities (PLCs) work, while Sommers had a deep history of work as a principal and staff developer. Their latest coauthored work offers insights into how collegial learning contributes to school success. The book emphasizes how school leaders can initiate and develop a PLC with their staffs. Hord and Sommers also include many useful chapter learning activities for you to incorporate into your repertoire of leadership thoughts and behaviors.

An Activity

In Chapter 1 we introduced Corson Middle School as an example of a failed culture change. In this chapter we explored Valleyfield and suggested that the principal there had set the events in motion that catalyzed success. Compare these two schools. How were they similar? How did they differ? Which is more like your school? How might you ensure that the results of your culture change efforts are more like those at Valleyfield?

ANALYZING YOUR SCHOOL

Diagnostic Resources

We offer several ways of collecting data within the school and thinking about your school culture. If you are thinking about using these, we recommend that you use them as separate tools, reflecting on each before beginning another.

A Quick School Culture Inventory

In our school . . .	SD	D	A	SA
Teachers are encouraged to share ideas.	1	2	3	4
Teachers trust each other.	1	2	3	4
Teachers support the philosophy of the school.	1	2	3	4
Teachers have common expectations for student performance.	1	2	3	4
Teachers spend considerable time planning together.	1	2	3	4
Teachers regularly seek ideas from colleagues.	1	2	3	4
Teachers are involved in the decision-making process.	1	2	3	4
Teachers take time to observe each other teaching.	1	2	3	4
Teachers value professional development.	1	2	3	4
Teachers value other teachers' ideas.	1	2	3	4
Teachers' work together is supported by the principal(s).	1	2	3	4
Teachers are kept informed about current issues in school.	1	2	3	4
Teachers and parents communicate frequently about student achievement and success.	1	2	3	4
Teachers are generally aware of what others are teaching.	1	2	3	4
Teachers maintain a current knowledge base about the learning process.	1	2	3	4
Teachers work cooperatively in groups.	1	2	3	4
Teachers work together to develop and evaluate programs and projects.	1	2	3	4
Teachers value school improvement.	1	2	3	4
Teachers who disagree about instructional approaches openly discuss their concerns.	1	2	3	4

Getting Wet: A Morning Analysis

Position yourself in a main location in the school to use this data collection tool.

List and evaluate the major features of the area in which you are standing:

Feature (briefly describe): _____

This feature . . .		
Warmly welcomes people to the building.	Yes	No
Offers direction to someone who may be new to the building.	Yes	No
Sets our school apart from others.	Yes	No
Conveys a sense of who we are as a school community.	Yes	No
Offers strong evidence this school is a place of learning.	Yes	No
Is purposeful.	Yes	No
Is well maintained.	Yes	No
Is remembered by others who visit our building.	Yes	No
Would be missed if it were to be moved or removed.	Yes	No
Has always been in this place.	Yes	No
Is relatively new to the school or this place in the school.	Yes	No
Is student created or features student work.	Yes	No

List and evaluate the interactions between others as they pass through the area in which you are standing.

People appear to be . . .		
Happy or cheerful	Yes	No
Grumpy or ill-tempered	Yes	No
Focused and inwardly oriented	Yes	No
Socially interacting with others about them	Yes	No
Professionally interacting with others about them	Yes	No
Alone	Yes	No
In small groups	Yes	No
In large groups	Yes	No
Mostly with others like them (e.g., students with students, girls with girls, boys with boys)	Yes	No
Mostly in mixed groups (e.g., teachers with students, parents with teachers, staff with faculty)	Yes	No

Reflect on the data you have collected.

Would others see this area in the same way you did?

How might their observations differ?

How might their observations agree with yours?

What do these data tell you about your school?

Are there any surprises in your observations?

How will you use these data as part of your cultural inventory?

Washing: Adding the Insights of Others

This activity is designed to help you work through the discovery phase of the appreciative inquiry process. It is best completed over time with a small core team of teachers and staff.

Each member of the team should talk with at least three other members of the school and have these questions answered. Try to collect examples and stories of the successful programs and practices in which teachers, students, and parents engage. When everyone has completed his or her interviews, complete the formal summary and discussion protocol that follows.

Questions:

1. What about this school makes you most proud? Why?

2. What about this school serves the students well? Why?

3. What about this school serves the faculty well? Why?

4. What about this school serves the parents and the community well? Why?

5. What about this school makes it unique? Why?

Formal Summary Protocol

Find a location in the school where a large piece of butcher paper can be hung.

Divide the paper into the following five columns.

Stories of Pride	Student Stories	Faculty Stories	Parent and Community Stories	Stories of Uniqueness

List in each column a brief synopsis of the story or example that the interview process collected.

Once each story or example is listed, look within each column. Reflect on the following questions.

Are there common themes to the stories?

Do the stories mention common topics, programs, policies, or ideas?

In what ways are they similar?

In what ways do they differ?

How might the stories be grouped? Try to find two or three common themes for each column.

Look across the columns. Reflect on these questions.

Are there common themes to the stories?

Do the stories mention common topics, programs, policies, or ideas?

In what ways are they similar?

In what ways do they differ?

How might the stories be grouped? Try to find two or three common themes for the entire collection.

Find a way to share these themes with others in the building. You might keep the butcher paper collection in a prominent location, use the stories in the school newsletter, or share them at staff meetings.

4

Linking Leadership and School Culture

In the previous chapter we discussed how to get a better understanding of your school's culture and how to engage others in that process. Even if you aren't ready for an elaborate diagnostic process, you will want to create some movement and direction. This chapter focuses on the theme of intensifying leadership through decision making and school improvement processes. While the pressures to do everything in a year (actually nine months) are enormous in most schools, culture change is usually protracted. Culture change is not merely a matter of knowledge or skill. The key to creating and maintaining culture change is in getting focused on important goals and involving others in achieving them.

In this chapter you will learn about:

- how decision making can be enhanced by intensifying leadership;
- how going slow involves making strategic choices;
- the importance of vigilance in maintaining strong school cultures;
- creating an organizational narrative that supports change efforts; and
- using school improvement as a strategy for promoting trust, communication, and risk taking.

LEADERSHIP AND DECISION MAKING

The focus of this book is on improving culture and intensifying leadership. At this juncture, the obvious needs restatement: a robust school culture is one in which leaders—both administrators and teachers—make daily decisions that will produce the long-run benefits for students. In the first chapter, we warned against thinking about culture change as a "quick fix," but we acknowledge that schools are dynamic, event-filled settings in which quick thinking and action is often necessary. An inevitable fact of school life is that, behind the routines, each shift in classroom activities and each encounter in the hall involves split-second judgments about what is the next best thing to do. In addition, every school is facing ongoing fundamental decisions about how to allocate resources, what projects are most worthy, and how to develop procedures that will be fair, just, and achievable.

Under these conditions, maintaining an eye on the long run has three advantages.

1. Long-run thinking focuses decision making on *core organizational issues and principles,* even when the decisions must be immediate. When John is taunting Susie in the hall, the principle of adults modeling the behavior they would like to see in students will affect the adults' reactions.

2. It preserves one's ability to *adapt and innovate* as needed. It is not the particular instructional program that is important, but what it is doing for student learning.

3. It provides leaders a way to build *coherent and consistent cultures* around what matters over time to the successes of the school and those that learn and work within. The result is that the rapid decisions each member must make without time to talk and reflect generally will promote "what matters most."

THE CASE OF YAHOO!

In November 2006, the *New York Times* ran an article suggesting that Yahoo! had lost its focus and, in turn, its edge in the search engine marketplace. The article accused the company of spreading itself too thinly, "like peanut butter on bread." By trying to be everything to everyone, the assertion was that they had lost sight of their central core. Rather than defend Yahoo!'s practices, Brad Garlinghouse, a Yahoo! senior vice president, responded with an organizational memo that was subsequently published in the *Wall Street Journal* (2006). In the memo he noted that the "measure of any person is not in how many times he or she falls down—but rather the spirit and resolve used to get back up." He then went on to agree with the core points the *Times* had made in their piece. Garlinghouse publicly suggested that Yahoo! suffered from three potentially fatal flaws. He claimed that Yahoo! lacked a focused, cohesive vision; clarity of ownership/ accountability; and decisiveness.

He argued that short-term Band-Aids could not provide the necessary direction for long-term quality decision making and choices. By reacting to others in the marketplace, Yahoo! lost the core of who they were and what they wanted to become. By "being peanut butter," the company had lost its focus. He called for himself and the rest of the management team to "boldly and definitively declare what we are and what we are not."

Doesn't this story reflect the issues that face many of today's schools? If we substituted the name of your school for Yahoo!, would you recognize yourself? Garlinghouse looked squarely at himself and noted that leadership was diffuse and uncertain, leading employees to question who was in charge and whether anyone cared about the decisions that got made in the course of a workday. When no one feels a sense of responsibility and ownership for the work, innovation and creativity are discouraged, both in business and in schools. Finally, he noted, "without a clear and focused vision . . . we lack a macro perspective to guide our decisions. . . . We are repeatedly stymied by challenging and hairy decisions. We are held hostage by our analysis paralysis" (*Wall Street Journal*, 2006, ¶16). The memo ends by noting that change is a marathon and not a sprint—short-term decisions will not lead to long-term success.

Leadership for the long run is evidenced by the actions leaders take in response to events as they arise. Garlinghouse responded publicly and forcefully because his company ended up in major business news reports. As a school leader, it is unlikely that you will need to make this kind of public response. However, at the core of his action he held the existing culture up to the light and determined that it was thin and weak. Whether Yahoo! fades into memory or is resurgent is not the important part of this story; what it tells us is that even good and exciting cultures can become tired, and that leadership is important in creating an environment for reinvigoration. Now let's consider a more ordinary school-based decision-making scenario.

THERE ARE NEVER ENOUGH RESOURCES

The technology team approached Joan Addams, principal of White High School, in her school with a request for new equipment for the computer lab. Excited by the initiative outlined in the proposal, she brought the request to her leadership group. They too were

(Continued)

(Continued)

impressed but felt that they should consider it in relation to other financial concerns facing the school. A shrinking tax-base had resulted in tighter budgets and additional oversight of discretionary spending; principals were instructed to maintain the essentials while trimming extras. The school had a small project account but funding the department's request would significantly reduce the flexibility to act on future requests. It might also create resentment among other departments. Nevertheless, Joan believed that some way must be found to support the request. The administrative group talked for most of the meeting about the proposal, raising several arguments to support or deny it. In the end of, they chose to table the decision in favor of requesting a new proposal—one more in keeping with the budgetary concerns facing the school.

On the surface the decision appears rather straightforward: *to fund or not to fund*? Like Garlinghouse at Yahoo!, Addams is faced with a dilemma that requires long-run thinking. At stake are decisions related to core missions of the department and school; relationships between staff and faculty, teachers, and students; and the use of scarce resources, to name a few. Making the decision, however, is further complicated by several contextual factors.

Decision Contexts and Rational Models

Decision context is an abstract concept subsuming a variety of factors that facilitate, constrain, and channel decision-making processes. It suggests elements such as the *setting* in which a decision emerges and is addressed; the *specific, immediate characteristics* of that setting (who is involved, what their interests are, etc.); and *how these features interact* to define and influence the process of making a decision. We often talk about "good decisions" or "bad decisions" when we look at what has happened at a particular school, but as these judgments are made we must take context into consideration. To give a simple example, moving a principal from one elementary school to another might be a good decision or a bad one, depending on the characteristics of the principals, the schools, and the community needs or demands, among other factors.

The decisions Garlinghouse faced at Yahoo! played out across the pages of major newspapers and required the company's leadership to confront its internal culture. In contrast, Addams has the luxury of semiprivacy because few outside the school are interested in the computer classroom. She faces, however, challenging internal pressures and values. Complex and multifaceted in nature, these decisions require more than the application of a problem-solving recipe.

Traditional management and planning texts usually presume a *rational model* of decision making. Rational decision-making models describe how decisions should be made assuming the presence of an omniscient decision maker making optimal choices under optimal conditions that include adequate information, a clear picture of decision preferences (preferred ends), and the ability to rank alternatives and assess their costs and benefits (March, 1988; Simon, 1976). They also assume that a competent leader is capable of juggling all the data, choices, and goals related to the decision at hand.

However, personal experience and several decades of research suggest that decision-making contexts in schools (and other organizations) rarely approach these conditions. Instead, decision contexts are messy—fraught with inadequate information, insufficient time, and scarce attention to long-term outcomes and consequences. Garlinghouse suggested that at Yahoo! disorganization and inefficiency were rampant, and he hoped to tidy up at least one part of it (attention to long-term goals). What is striking about straightforward meetings such as those of Joan Addams's team is how disorganized they often are and how broadly the discussion can range given that everyone thought they were there to rubber-stamp a proposal. When decision-making opportunities arise, it is difficult for members to focus and prioritize. Discussion can swing back and forth between issues of real importance and trivial matters of administrative detail. Irrelevant data is confused for useful and purposeful information. Learning is often truncated, and as a result trust may be undermined rather than built.

Garbage Cans and Compost

Rather than intensifying leadership with the intent of developing *more leadership* leading to *consistent or communal action*, organizational theorists Cohen, March, and Olsen (1972) argue that organizations often become mired in difficulties such as those outlined above due to several common characteristics:

- *An ambiguity of goals* characterized by inconsistent and ill-defined preferences and a multiplicity of objectives. When goals are unclear, few issues can be resolved by appealing to shared priorities. Decision making flounders not because people aren't working hard, but because they are working on the wrong things.
- *Ambiguous processes* for decision making, goal attainment, and working together. Schools struggle because the activities to be performed are rarely unambiguous. Instead of following a clear and focused path, members' actions are based on a combination of experience, trial and error, imitation, and inventions born of necessity. Unclear processes can lead to "learning disabilities" and long learning curves (Senge, 1990).
- *Fluid participation* marked by variable commitments of time and effort. Sometimes members will focus solely on their own work, leaving decisions to others; at other times, they may be very

concerned with particular organizational matters and want to be involved. The issues being addressed, the choices to be made, and timing and personal temperament often determine the degree of participation.

- *Most decisions are of low significance* for most members, which leads to inertia. Even important decisions may secure only partial attention from teachers and team members; often the attention devoted to a particular issue is tied less to its content than its symbolic significance and its impact on group esteem. Consequently, there is a tendency to continue with the policies and procedures of the past.
- Finally, there is a *weak information base*. The data necessary for informed decision making is not consistently collected (perhaps because of the unclear processes) and often not well disseminated (in part due to the fluidity of participation).

We're sure at this juncture you're beginning to wonder how decisions get made at all in circumstances such as these. Again Cohen, March, and Olsen help us to understand. They suggest that decision making in many organizations functions like a *garbage can*. In a garbage can process, a large number of ubiquitous and unresolved issues or problems all get tossed in, to be addressed by the volunteers who are willing to take them on. In Joan Addams's case, the unresolved issue was the purpose and procedures related to the special projects fund, and a few staff members could volunteer to clarify these. Other issues get dragged in when schools discuss the simplest questions including student behavior, achievement and progress, space and resource allocations, staffing and budget concerns, as well more routine matters such as bus schedules and lunchroom duties. Furthermore, in many schools busy leaders can rely on a stock set of solutions that have worked well in the past—forming a committee to look at the matter further, offering a broad range of in-service and workshop offerings, or, as in Joan Addams's case, tabling the issue until its implications could be considered.

All of these conditions—the omnipresent nature of problems, the variety of potential choices, ready solutions—are tangled together in the decision context. As a result, problems are rarely addressed comprehensively, and they keep reappearing when temporary or partial solutions run their course. Furthermore, the more issues a school deals with and the more complexity those issues involve, the more likely that the same problem will be recycled. No wonder teachers often feel that "we've tried to fix that before, but nothing works."

Because March's "garbage can" phenomenon is so prevalent, we need to think about other ways to lead a decision-making process. In the best case, messy "garbage" is recycled as mingled and enriched compost; provisional solutions are refined, clarified, and made more permanent. Clear focus, accountability, and decisiveness help to make compost from many of the issues that comprise the soup of awaiting and unresolved decisions. However, without the concerted effort of a team of people following through on decision-making plans and outcomes, improvement is unlikely to occur. In this way, if we think about intensified leadership as *changing the way in which decisions are made* and *deciding which decisions are on the table*, our enduring problems become fodder for real and lasting change. We turn now to considering the issue of how leaders can present and frame decision-making and school-improvement opportunities, as well as how to use these opportunities as they arise to strengthen school cultures.

INTENSIFYING LEADERSHIP AT YOUR SCHOOL

Intensifying leadership suggests that schools must first look within for the resources to improve outcomes. More leadership from more people is not a goal in itself, but is one of the means of enriching your opportunities and potential for improving learning processes and outcomes. By focusing on the *processes of leadership*—problem finding, decision making, solution testing—instead of the *tasks of leaders*—developing budgets, creating schedules and calendars, student support and behavior—the foundation of intensified leadership is rooted in the interactions between school organization members.

Simply put, intensifying leadership requires skills and responsibilities to be developed across a critical mass of organizational members. Involving a broader group of people in diagnosing your organization culture, as was suggested in the previous chapter, can be seen as an important first step in intensification, and a good diagnosis will result in a long list of "issues" or decision opportunities that people want to address. It will not lead to real change unless the sense of commitment and involvement that was generated is turned toward working on key decisions.

Intensified leadership should not be confused with delegation or coordination of activities. Delegation may diversify the number of people involved in carrying out school activities but it does not necessarily lead to the collective work that fosters learning and trust. Things may get done but rarely does anyone have ownership in the completed whole. Most teachers have had experiences with the kind of "shared leadership" in which tasks are shifted away from the principal's office, but decisions continue to be made at the top or by a small number of people. In contrast, intensified leadership suggests that members work together to address the teaching and learning needs of the school by adopting and employing:

- shared, communally held goals,
- based on collective values and beliefs, and
- by using mutually understood methods of problem finding and resolution.

In this way, school culture is enhanced as the role of leadership is shared among members and reinforced through interactions between teachers, parents, students, and the community.

Intensified Leadership and Management

One of the immediate benefits of intensified leadership is that it allows the school community to broaden the number of people involved in running the school. Distributing management tasks also provides leaders with an opportunity to capitalize on opportunities for enhancing existing school culture. Leadership consists of taking action to promote behaviors that stimulate improvement. We have suggested that the opportunities for management and leadership cannot always be anticipated. In many ways, they are circumstance dependent and contextual in nature. However, we do not believe that school leaders need to sit back and wait for opportunities to arise. By creating the conditions that both seek out opportunities for growth and excellence and enhance the capacity of the school to respond to opportunity as it arises, intensified leadership fosters positive school culture.

FOCUSING ON ASSESSMENT AT MILLERSWOOD HIGH

MHS is a typical large comprehensive high school. On entering the school, a visitor would immediately note the way the school's hallways fanned out from the central core of the building. It was designed in the late 1990s, and each wing was built to house a complete department including classrooms, labs, conference rooms, and teachers' offices and meeting areas. As a result, in the early years of the school's operation, though students traveled the building throughout their day, most teachers rarely left their subject-separated wings. Not surprisingly, a teacher's closest and most trusted colleagues could usually be found two or three doors down from their own room. With each passing year, as enrollment numbers climbed, a few more teachers would be pressured to leave their wing and take a room in a less crowded area of the building. For some, leaving the protection of their closest colleagues was threatening and difficult, but others welcomed the opportunity for interdisciplinary conversation. They noted that talking about students they had in common was easier and that they enjoyed talking and working with "folks who didn't always see they world like I did." The school administrative team watched the slow evolution of the school's culture as it changed from one of isolated separatists to a more collegial environment. Finally, after three years of this slow change, the principal suggested that the wing structure had run its course and he was thinking about fully integrating the school. His suggestion was met with wide support.

Revisiting the yin-yang diagram that we first presented in Chapter 2 may help to clarify what we mean (Figure 4.1). Creating the conditions for unexpected discoveries means that principals need to keep the tasks identified as part of cultural leadership and cultural management in mind—and they need to make sure that others have the freedom to explore their own work within the same framework. To give an example: Only when staff members are alert to the potential for listening and reacting to events that suggest that working within the current paradigm isn't always working (cultural management) will you be able to identify what people are already doing, on the ground, that may suggest a new paradigm. This is what already happens in the best team meetings: Teachers bring a problem that they are encountering to the table and others who have the same problem share what they have done differently that seems to work. The experimentation that follows can, if minds are open, lead to change that reflects both leadership and management.

INTENSIFYING LEADERSHIP BY BUILDING PCOLT

Commitment to intensifying leadership (and management) within your school requires reconsidering your current images of leadership. Leaders who aspire to be heroes, bosses, or superior(s) need not apply. Intensifying leadership demands that you actively seek the help and support of others, building school cultures that rely on the wisdom of the many (Surowiecki, 2004). However, intensified leadership will not magically happen in schools. It requires thoughtfulness about *who* is encouraged to take on *what* tasks. It requires that all the right people be engaged in work that they are well suited to complete. So how does a leader think about who should do what things? We submit that leaders should draw on the research that has been completed in the past decade on professional community, organizational learning, and trust, or PCOLT. When considered together these ideas offer school leaders the means to achieve school improvement goals and ends.

Principals who have developed schools where PCOLT flourishes share the following characteristics:

- *Collective identity* based on shared values, beliefs, and direction. A sense of common purpose binds members through an explicit recognition of what matters most. By knowing the *direction* the school is headed (a term that we think is more realistic than the more common terms of *mission* and *vision*) and the ways in which they intend to get there (including professional development, instructional initiatives, and governance practices, to name a few avenues), common identity can catalyze participation in leadership.
- *Focus on learning* where the primary activity is on improving outcomes for students. Other activities, ranging from collaborations

Figure 4.1   Cultural Management and Leadership in Schools

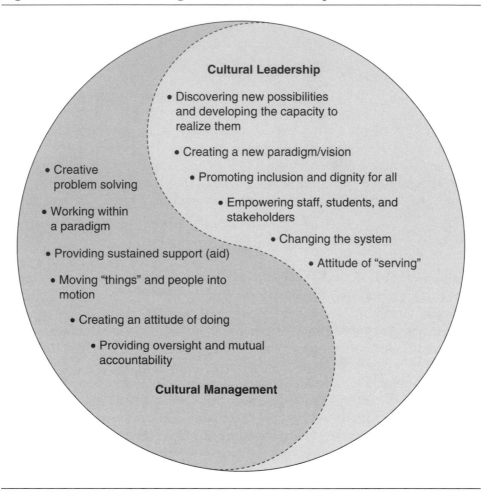

SOURCE: Adapted from M. Schratz. (2003). From administering to leading a school. *Cambridge Journal of Education, 33*(3), 408.

with community agencies to developing a specialized curriculum focus are nice, but they should be clearly viewed as a means to the primary end. In traditional school settings, the focus is on individual learning for students but also for teachers. In schools where PCOLT is present, individual learning leads to shared understandings and collective action toward goals. The pervasive nature of learning within the school is reinforced by ongoing reflection and inquiry that is embedded in the daily work of the faculty and staff.

- *Philosophy of contribution* where power and authority are shared across the school, and diversity in ways of thinking about problems is encouraged. Contributions may vary across individuals, where some members serve in mentoring or coaching roles, others provide expertise in data collection and analysis, and still others serve in formal governance roles. The overall effect is one in which not everyone is engaged in every aspect of an improvement agenda but all are engaged in contributing toward shared success.

- *Trust* provides the "superglue" that holds school communities together. Without internal trust, faculty and staff cannot engage in the necessary work to improve student-learning outcomes. It also requires leaders to trust that solutions arrived at by others will be better than those they could dream up themselves. Without external trust, a school's relationship with the community is at best tenuous and the school may be unable to generate support for student learning efforts. Trust provides the foundation on which members are willing to risk the public display of their practice and thinking. Furthermore, trust provides needed springboards for the development of innovative practice and improvement.

To have a vibrant culture requires that all of these be present; if they are not, serious distortions of purpose may occur. If we look at the case of Lakeview, we see a school that had a strong collective identity and a great deal of accumulated trust, but lacked the other key ingredients (this case is adapted from Zwicky, 2008).

LAKEVIEW SCHOOL AND A TRADITION OF SOLIDARITY

Lakeview Elementary has served the same working-class urban community for more than eighty years. Originally a mixed-race neighborhood, riots in the 1970s caused most white families to move to an abutting suburb, but the remaining African American families (and a newer group of Asians) remained loyal to the school. Many parents had also gone to Lakeview and had fond memories of their days at the school. With a very stable staff, it was common for children to be taught by the same teachers their parents had.

A merger with another school and the shock of racially disaggregated achievement scores (before No Child Left Behind) created some dissatisfactions, and Principal Artie Simmons, who was the school's benevolent leader for nearly twenty years, decided to retire. Without his calming presence, other issues began to emerge, though they were not discussed. Parents chose to move their children to new charter schools, which promised better and more culturally sensitive learning environments, and enrollment dropped by nearly one-third. There were outstanding teachers who were recognized by the district as leaders in raising student achievement and engaging parents. They rarely talked, however, to the many teachers who had happily spent their whole career at the school, but who were less successful in adapting to the district's new literacy programs. Little had changed within Lakeview, but everything was changing around it.

When a new principal, who made it clear that she did not fully trust the staff to do the best for students, arrived, Lakeview began to fall apart. Two years later, the district decided to close the school.

SOURCE: This case is adapted from Cindy Zwicky. (2008). *Pushed or pulled? Between school mobility among experienced teachers*. PhD dissertation, University of Minnesota, Minneapolis.

The big question is how to build school cultures rich in all the PCOLT attributes. Principals cannot simply exhort teachers and community members to share a collective identity. Nor can they easily mend broken-trust environments, refocusing all eyes on teaching and learning. Building PCOLT takes time because it is the core work of culture change. However it is marked by clear and easily recognized shifts in focus, behavior, and action. When schools shift from low PCOLT environments to schools in which leadership is intensified and contributes to PCOLT, the following differences can be observed.

Table 4.1   Indicators of High and Low PCOLT

	Low PCOLT Settings	*High PCOLT Settings*
Collective Identity		
	No clear focus on expectations to guide shared work.	Common foci on expectations and goals.
	Individual ideas about how the school should operate.	Shared norms and values about practice.
	Teachers problem solve on their own.	Teachers work together to address problems of practice—ongoing discussions learning from others.
Focus on Learning		
	Classroom doors are closed.	Practice is public.
	Staff turnover and/or conflict prevent memory from assisting change.	Staff develop shared memories (both positive and negative) to assist new learning and change.
	Inconsistent and/or specialized professional development.	Staff creates both individual and shared expertise.
	No systematic measures of progress.	Measures of progress are shared and understood by all staff.

	Low PCOLT Settings	*High PCOLT Settings*
Philosophy of Contribution		
	Focus on individual power, authority, and control.	Shared leadership roles and expectations.
	Centrally located decision making.	Participative decision making.
	Contrived or pseudo collegiality; false participation in activities.	Pervasive and voluntary focus on teaching and learning goals.
Trust		
	Staff are isolated or in fragmented competing groups.	Staff are cooperative and collaborative with a strong community identity.
	Proliferation of rules to control behavior.	Facilitative rules designed to solve problems.
	Constrained communication around trivial matters.	Open and reflective dialogue about core issues of school improvement.
	Decisions made by one group are frequently disregarded or undermined by others.	Decentralized decision making is almost always accepted.
	External community is disengaged or only marginally engaged with the school.	External community is engaged and integrated with the school.

Now that we have shared a sense of what a PCOLT culture looks like in practice, we turn our attention to thinking about how leaders can use these ideas to intensify leadership efforts within their schools. We focus our discussion on the ways in which intensified leadership can help to enhance PCOLT efforts. Like the real estate success cliché (i.e., location, location, location), intensified leadership can be thought of as communication, communication, and communication (Schneider & Hollenczer, 2006). Communication includes *who* you include (internal and external stakeholders), *what* you talk about (beliefs, values, directions, and outcomes), and *when* (time, place, and spanning boundaries) you participate in the discussion.

It's What You Say *and* How You Say It

When we visit schools, it rarely takes more than a few minutes before someone begins to outline an ambitious agenda for school improvement, pointing to a variety of workshops, programs, and adoptions. In almost every case, the amount of time it will take to accomplish the goals is underestimated. One of our favorite research findings (which has never been published) was from a study of urban high schools engaged in ambitious comprehensive reform activities in the 1980s (Louis & Miles, 1990). A survey of a national sample of principals in these schools revealed a surprising finding: The longer they had been involved in working on reform activities, the longer they thought it would take until they had accomplished their goals! Those who were in the first year or so thought they were be "done" in a few more years; those that had been at it for four or five years indicated that they would need another four or five. This finding supports our observation that ambitious leaders rarely realistically consider how they will get to their goals. Consider each of these brief examples of new principals and their handling of the first-day, start-of-the-school-year meeting.

TWO NEW PRINCIPALS: SAME MESSAGE, DIFFERENT DELIVERY

Tim Andersen was promoted to high-school principal after years at the middle school. When his first faculty meeting began, he took fifteen minutes to introduce himself to his new staff and outlined how he planned to continue the excellent tradition of academic achievement the high school had established. He ended his presentation by stating his goal that learning "for every kid, in every class, every day" would be his focus. He then invited the teachers to offer their own thoughts on how these goals might be achieved and the ways in which they might participate in achieving them. Finally, he scheduled another meeting in which these (and other) new ideas could be discussed and ultimately implemented.

David James was promoted from assistant principal to principal when his district opened a new middle school. The opening ran smoothly, and when the staff came together for the first time, James thanked them for their hard work and announced, "Student learning is important to me, and here are some ideas about what we need to do this year and in the future." Then he distributed a double-sided single sheet of paper titled "The Strategic Learning Plan" to all the teachers and asked that they read it carefully. The counseling staff examined the policy for student schedule changes, but few teachers reviewed it because they were busy with back-to-school activities. By Halloween, it had all but been forgotten.

Both Andersen and James delivered the message that student learning mattered, putting a lot of effort into impressive plans to back up their sentiments. However, Andersen understood that how he framed his goals as action opportunities was important. James did not. Andersen understood that the how he delivered the message would have an impact on carrying out the substance of his initiatives. James assumed that teachers would know how to act. The level of activity in Andersen's school as staff moved toward shaping the larger plan was palpable; in James's school, the faculty barely paid attention to what was expected of them.

Style Matters

It is easy to think of cultural leadership style as a superficial "charm school" substitution for the substance of what we do. Certainly the *what* of school improvement has to be gotten right, and it involves many important decisions about curriculum and instruction, teaching, and learning. However, the ways in which we approach problem solving and decision making, and how we implement our choices, is significant as well. Style helps to create the cultural context in which we work.

Approach Matters

When leaders step up and make the most of simple opportunities (such as the usual "honeymoon" afforded new principals, or the general excitement that accompanies the opening of the school year), they can change the reality of the school's culture. Seeing and making use of opportunity requires the ability to get out in front of the issue and explaining it so that others clearly understand what can be done and what part they will play. When Tim Andersen framed his school improvement message, he did so in a way that allowed teachers to see themselves as part of the change because his presentation had practical implications but did not present a set of "marching orders." When he talked about "every kid, every class, every day," he spoke with an authentic voice, and his invitation to join in showed leadership by example rather than by authority.

Timing Matters

Years ago, the *New Yorker* magazine ran a cartoon of an executive sitting behind his desk ordering a subordinate to "Get me a new corporate culture, by Monday." The cartoon was funny for two reasons—first because of the poke it takes at businesses executives ready to jump on the latest fad seemingly without any understanding of the issues involved. The second is the speed with which he wants change to occur. We've said this before, but it's worth repeating: Culture change takes time. A lot of it. When people think about timing, they usually consider *when* something ought to be done rather than *how long* it will take. Smart leaders come to culture change understanding that transformation requires diagnosing current artifacts, norms, and values, but also focusing on an emerging consensus about what should take their place.

Storytelling

We have suggested that a school's culture is created by the values, artifacts, and underlying assumptions of those who work and learn there (Chapter 3). While some of these are obvious to all, others are less easily observed and understood. One way to communicate the important aspects of your school culture is to encourage storytelling.

Stories help to bind people together and, for this reason, are pervasive in our lives. Think about how you share the details of your day when you arrive home or how you catch up with an old friend: You tell stories. At times those stories are painstakingly detailed descriptions of what occurred, while at other times you touch only on a few highlights. In either case, you share the story so that another person can understand your experience of what happened. Some families have tales that get told for generations. Stories allow us to know who we are and where we have come from.

Schools too, have a cultural history. We tell stories about who we were as an organization, and how that affects what we are today. We might be the school who raised enough money to build a new playground in just one week, or we might be the school who struggled but was successful in implementing block scheduling. Sometimes stories are about decline, like the one that the teachers who anticipated Lakeview Elementary's closure recounted. When the school's story is told, members can share a common perspective concerning "who we are."

Stories of success, achievement, and accomplishment help to positively strengthen school cultures, but can also blind members to emerging weaknesses. Conversely, *stories of disappointment* and failure can reinforce negative school cultures, but in some cases are parts of a larger story of revitalization against the odds. Stories can serve to help preserve the culture of the school, but they also serve to build bridges with the past and future. *Transformation stories* help school leaders craft a vision for the future. Stories can be used to inspire change, foster increased collaboration, share existing knowledge with others, and spark action. The challenge for school leaders is to know the stories that are already being told, find a compelling new story to tell, and then recount it in a way that inspires others. Simply put, they need to find the right story and then tell it right. You do not need to do this alone. Sometimes a principal who is not the best storyteller in the school can take advantage of the local raconteur, who can engage everyone in the details of story.

Telling the right story suggests that you are transmitting a vision for the school. It must connect the school's current reality to the future, honoring the faculty and staff, students, and community for the work they have already completed and still focuses them on the work still to come (see the discussion of appreciative inquiry in Chapter 3). By connecting the past to the future, the story helps members to see how the school can grow and change. The right story must also be understandable. It has to create learning within the mind of the listener so that new ideas are understood, acknowledged, and accepted. People must be able to make meaning of the story and to relate it to themselves.

Telling the story right suggests that you know what you want to say and that your message is simple enough for people to remember it. Stories that are too long or have too many distinct plot lines are often too hard for modern people (who have lost the oral tradition) to remember. Clear stories focus attention on the message of the story rather than the storyteller. When stories are focused, details and values remain consistent and truthful.

Stories also enhance decision making. James March (1988) proposed that decision making is influenced not only by how we calculate the consequences of our actions (the "rational" part of decision making), but is also influenced by identity, or how we think that others like us might make the same choice. Rather than asking how much time a meeting might take, how much a workshop costs, or how hard something is to accomplish, we ask as well, "What kind of a situation is this? And what do people like me do in situations like this one?" In this second case, values and principles balance rational calculations. Our identity is formed and reinforced by the stories we choose to tell; in turn, our decision-making choices are informed by our stories.

Stories are effective teaching tools. That's why we have peppered this book with real-life vignettes that we hope will help you to think and will motivate you to reflect on your work. Selecting stories involved a lot of thinking on our part: What did we want to communicate? What experiences with school cultures were most important to share? Stories ask each of us—the teller and the listener—to be active in constructing meaning and in generating more questions. When using stories to enhance school culture, it is important to think about the intention for telling the story. Do you mean to convey a sense of identity? Or do you mean to lead people to evaluate the consequences of their actions?

Thinking About Timing

You can work to create opportunities, but they cannot be forced. Timing and readiness make a difference. To capitalize on issues as they present themselves, you must be ready to act, calling on your ad hoc leadership and management skills). Readiness also implies that, rather than moving quickly, being slower but more strategic will, in the end, produce the results you seek. The garbage can has time to become compost. We offer several important benefits of slowing down to create more enduring culture change:

- *Exploring options.* It is not necessary to adopt every best practice that comes along, and discussing a variety of options is useful if you use it as an opportunity to reflect on those that are most central to the work you are doing.

- *Involving others.* Consulting with internal and external community members will increase ownership rather than mere buy-in. This may be particularly important if you are involving parents with divergent views.
- *Understanding potential outcomes.* Going slower allows time to think through not only the intended consequences, but also to observe and reflect on unintended consequences that emerge when change is in motion. People will react in unexpected ways, areas of resistance will appear or fall away, and the external environment may shift.
- *Creating real understanding.* Collecting good data takes time, but dependable data will help with future decisions and create a solid foundation for the next steps.

Some ways to slow down:

- *Clarify goals.* When goals are clear, they act as filters to sort through options and allow you to more easily maneuver around those that may be less central. When goals are clear, it is easier to encourage the leadership of others, because you can trust that they are on the same page. When efforts are consistently assessed against goals, your actions can be deliberate and intentional—and easier to explain to others as well.
- *Think—then respond.* School leaders are faced with hundreds of decision-making opportunities each day. Do not be afraid of appearing indecisive if you do not respond to each one instantly (which almost always means doing whatever is required yourself). Each represents a chance to shape the culture of your school, intensify leadership, and reinforce your goals.
- *Choose fewer initiatives,* and pare down those that create overload. It is impossible to manage a half-dozen efforts that are not clearly part of a whole. By all means, encourage experimentation. But some experiments become energy-consuming black holes and need to be eliminated. By continuously streamlining the school's work into better-aligned and deliberate efforts, everyone can concentrate their efforts on what matters.
- *Ignore the school calendar.* The school year has a clear beginning and an end, and educators become trapped in the same nine-month start-stop pattern that students face. Culture change doesn't fit neatly into these boundaries.

Considering *Who* Does *What*

One of the first tasks, even for an experienced school leader, is to create a fresh leadership inventory for the school. This involves identifying different types of leadership and mapping the involvement of all players in the school and community. Understanding *who* is doing *what* is a precondition to distributing or intensifying the leadership available for improvement. More than likely you already have a cadre of teachers, parents, and community members who serve as trusted advisors. You may seek the advice of Lily on issues related to instruction and curriculum, Mike when you need to talk about student support and behavior, or Chris when the issue is assessment. You already know who is open to thinking about changed instruction and who can be counted on to raise the hard but useful questions regarding new directions. These are the people on whom the foundations of intensifying school leadership rest. Many may view your patterns of consultation as sensible, but others often will see them as favoritism. In many cases, there are others who are willing and talented, should you call on them. This particularly struck us in a project that involved infusing arts education into the core subject matter and creating teaching partnerships with practicing artists.

WAYLAND ELEMENTARY SCHOOL AND ARTS-INFUSED EDUCATION

As teachers and the principal at Wayland, an inner-city elementary school with many immigrant children, discussed how they wanted to enrich students' experience in the arts, they discovered all sorts of talents among the staff. Of course they expected that several of them played the piano, but no one knew that Joan had once trained as an opera singer before switching to a more "practical" undergraduate degree, or that Bill made lutes in his spare time. Two teachers were involved in fabric arts and another was an accomplished watercolorist.

They began the work thinking that they would need to rely solely on their artist partners to develop curriculum and teaching strategies, using a "visiting artist" model. They ended up by engaging in a true collaboration between their own staff and the "real" artists in developing, delivering, and assessing the results of arts infusion.

The principal went on to write a proposal for district approval for Wayland's designation as an "Arts Community School," and they obtained several grants to continue their development work. The teachers' own data gathering suggested that the children from recently immigrated families were, in particular, gaining a great deal from opportunities to use alternative ways of expressing themselves in multiple ways as they learned to read and write in a foreign language.

Of course it is not surprising that people might not know about the avocations and the deep past of all other staff members, but Wayland's open process gave the staff a hint that there were probably other things that they did not know about each other as resources. The arts-infusion activity formed the basis for a tight, emerging professional community focused on alternative instruction in reading and mathematics. Teachers in Wayland—and teachers in your school—can happily take on a variety of leadership roles:

• *Professional development, including modeling, mentoring, and coaching.* Well-designed and conducted professional development can result in improved practice and student learning (Desimone, Porter, & Garet, 2002). External providers cannot, however, resolve the wide array of implementation challenges that emerge after even the best in-service offerings. In schools where classroom practice is public, modeling, mentoring, and coaching become important ways to support new practices. Like learning yoga postures, it helps to have someone else looking and making adjustments—even advanced practitioners have a guru or two. As in yoga, modeling creates exemplars of what best practice looks like in a real setting. Peer mentoring allows individuals to support each other and works particularly well in teams that already respect each other's practice and are willing to share. Coaching, on the other hand, is specific and skills focused, and it requires the coach to have an advanced level of expertise in order to provide feedback and advice. Care must be taken, of course, to avoid "contrived collegiality" in which mentoring and coaching are imposed by administrators (Hargreaves & Dawe, 1990).

• *Structured participation.* Structured participation focuses effort on increasing the arenas in which people can influence the school. These may be in governance and decision-making bodies, but more fruitful are the development of quality assurance and assessment teams, as well as regularized visioning and strategic planning efforts. Creating committees and teams that focus on the school's future recognizes that decision making related to shaping teaching and learning can be distinguished from managerial considerations. Additionally, faculty and professional staff are in the best position to shape and implement decisions related to matters of curriculum.

• *Problem finding.* Problem finding includes the cognitive processes and organizational practices that engage members in anticipating what might be going wrong and thus preparing to avert crises. Decision making occurs when a problem is agreed on and choices are made about how to deal with it. A problem can be found whenever there is a difference between what actually happens and what the school community wants to have happen, but many of these divergences are subtle. Unless problem finding is rewarded, the tendency is to ignore accumulating evidence; if staff fears a negative response when little problems are raised, they will turn away until the last moment.

• *Decision making.* No one wants a two-hour meeting to decide that the custodian needs to sweep the halls after the last lunch; a two-hour meeting cannot resolve a complex problem like developing a curriculum map for a subject in which there are no state and district standards. Simply put, decision processes should match the nature of the problems. Including others at a point when their contributions are meaningful and of significance to them is the most effective way of intensifying leadership.

• *Assessment of pedagogy and teaching resources.* School self-assessment, as part of a plan of improvement, can provide insight into whether policy and practices are working, as they should. In our experience, teachers do not mind being assessed as long as they have participated in setting the standards, trust that the person doing the assessment is competent, and believe that the purpose is improvement rather than punishments and rewards. By answering the question, "Did this work as intended?" leaders may learn where small corrections are needed or how new ideas are flawed. Evaluation, as a primary focus of intensified leadership, may be used to judge the effectiveness of a program or policy.

VIGILANCE AND STRONG SCHOOL CULTURES

In Chapter 1 we discussed the notion of strong, nimble cultures that demonstrate cohesive values and beliefs, as well as the ability to respond productively when conditions change. Just as the creation of strong culture requires attention and care, maintaining nimble cultures requires vigilance. We turn to a school that despite enjoying such a culture lost sight of its foundations.

CULTURE CONFLICT AT RED LAKE

Principal John Segner was very much at the helm of Red Lake Middle School. Shortly after he came, he led the faculty through a difficult decision to eliminate tracking and to initiate a four-period day. Teachers deeply appreciated his ability to create an atmosphere that valued faculty skills and knowledge. Segner focused his energy in three areas: providing internal intellectual resources for teachers to gain new insights into their practice, providing financial resources for them to attend outside courses and workshops, and empowering them to develop their passions through curriculum and instructional processes. Though teachers had considerable autonomy in designing their course content, there was a critical process of peer review of all proposed courses each term. Many courses were team taught, and teachers actively collaborated on their instruction during common, seventy-minute planning periods. The underlying assumption was that the strong professional community and respect among the staff results in collective agreements to which everyone was accountable.

After five years of experience with the new structures, an external review raised concerns about curriculum coordination. Segner decided, and the faculty agreed, that a committee should look into the issue. Volunteers, including parents and students, were chosen. They worked for a year, and eventually called a meeting to share the results of their study. As Segner remembers, the meeting was less than a rousing success: "It was real clear that nobody wanted anything to do with this, and nobody wanted to look at major huge change right now, again. Some people were interested in doing some study groups—so they said. But when it came time to have people sign up to do the study groups, nobody particularly wanted to sign up." Another meeting to revisit the committee's recommendations promoted a similarly negative response, and the curriculum revision initiative was disbanded. Several teachers who were not on the committee that celebrated Red Lake's success in creating the curriculum choice options prepared a report. John Segner left the school a year later.

Why was the curriculum committee different from the school's previous successful experiences with change? First, not all staff agreed that there was a real problem. The principal believed that there was a problem, and he was eager to get moving on the discussion process that had previously worked so well to promote the kind of continuous learning and change that he valued. However, by focusing on implementing a process that had worked in the past, Segner missed subtle cultural changes that had emerged at Red Lake. In spite of their cohesiveness and the level of teacher empowerment in the school, subcultures were beginning to appear. Newer teachers mentioned that they were less influential than teachers who had been there for many years; language arts faculty believed that they had larger workloads than other faculty; the process of student choice in course selection meant that some faculty had many more students than others.

Second, Segner took the open, inquiring culture of his school for granted. Though he reapplied a previously successful process to the curriculum problem, he failed to manage the change in a way that honored the cultural values that had become apparent: individualism and choice were central, and staff expected big issues to be resolved by debate and all-school discussion, and not by committees. When Segner's attention to the culture of the school faltered, the culture itself deteriorated. When he failed to engage the staff in a discussion about the current norms of behavior that bound faculty and staff together, the foundation on which the culture was build crumbled.

Finally, while the curriculum committee labored at their task, they did not engage other members of the school community, nor did they offer substantive updates as to what they were thinking. By spending too long in the "wash" phase, they isolated themselves from the larger school culture. Had they moved on to "rinse" by sharing their ideas with the broader school community, they might have gained support for and insight into how their ideas and plans would be received. Vigilance, the act of careful watching, requires school leaders to be alert to threats that can undermine their culture. Threats can come from within or from the outside. Each has the potential to disrupt an otherwise well-functioning school environment. However, it is not enough that the principal alone maintains a vigilant stance toward the shared values of the school. When leadership is intensified, members of the school community can work together to protect the culture they have created. Just as culture is created within the group, the group must maintain it. The trick is in realizing this too, is important.

CONCLUSION

In this chapter we have offered several vignettes. We examined difficulties at Yahoo!, White High School, and Lakeview Elementary. We described how leadership was intensified through PCOLT at Wayland Elementary, and we followed a culture change at Red Lake Middle School. In each of these cases, both the formal leaders and others played a role in creating and shaping culture, and throughout the chapter we have considered how the need for intensified leadership interacts with the imperative of focusing on student learning. The vignettes differed; together they can offer us insight into common mistakes, which we share each here:

- *Mistaking activities for outcomes.* By confusing "doing" with strategically focused effort, they confuse the means with the ends. When means are confused with ends, focus is centered on the activity, rather than the results it was intended to create. When schools rely on checking innovations off the list (yep, we did that one), whatever change is created by these efforts is short-lived and often ineffective. Without a strategic focus on the intended outcome, effort is wasted and unproductive.
- *Mistaking the creation of new systems for innovation.* Another form of "doing" is restructuring to address long-standing school tensions and dilemmas. When school leaders attempt to create policies and systems to address what are really issues of the school culture (e.g., how we treat each other), we often limit rather than expand our creative possibilities. When the underlying assumptions that inform systems and structures, policy and practice, are not surfaced, the new systems and structures do no better than the ones they replaced. This is because the real issue (the culture) was not addressed.
- *Mistaking planning, talking, reading, and thinking for accomplishments.* Unlike the schools that adopt every innovation that comes their way, some schools have cultures where endless discussion is the norm. These schools are littered with book clubs, formal and informal committees, and meetings and retreats that in the end produce ideas that fail to be implemented. By mistaking the generation of new ideas with efforts and practices that are at the heart of cultural change, opportunities are lost and members become discouraged with and disengaged from the school.
- *Mistaking the creative efforts of a few for shared success.* When individuals rather than teams of teachers, parents, and leaders work on projects, the only learning that can occur is individual learning. While creative efforts may result, learning does not. When the school organization fails to learn its ability to retain and enhance these efforts is decreased.

On the other hand, where change efforts are successful, school leaders set an agenda for change. Scholars of culture suggest that a change agenda can be established and supported by the following:

- *Emphasizing to everyone that change is an ongoing process.* Big and small change results when members of the school community accept the fact that current programs and practices are not adequate to address the needs of current students and the community. As students and surrounding communities continue to evolve, so must you. In this way, we are never "done" with the change process; small and large corrections to the system must always be considered.

- *Keeping everyone's sights on clear and focused outcomes.* Change without a clear end in mind can result in unintended and potential damaging outcomes for a school's culture. By naming the goals for which you are reaching, it is both easier to distinguish the means to get you there as well as to filter out distractions.

- *Developing intelligent and focused data collection tools.* Once goals and ends are clear, they find ways in which meaningful data provides information regarding progress. It is not necessary to have file cabinets full of reports; rather, several reliable and trustworthy sources are all that is necessary. The trick is to collect and analyze the data on hand and to use it to make corrections to plans as needed.

- *Identifying measures of success.* Principals, in concert with the staff, find both short- and long-term ways to mark progress. The attainment of short-term goals allows you to celebrate small wins, allowing you to intensify effort and energy for future work. When measures are in place for long-term gain, regular assessment of school processes and practices can be institutionalized.

- *Involving others in the work.* Not only is it easier to create change when others assist in the effort, but by involving others—teachers, staff, parents, and community—it is also easier to develop a broad base of support for change.

- *Identifying barriers to and facilitators of change.* Every change effort is fraught with those issues and people who can stand in the way of your plans. Similarly, a raft of supporting players and resources exist as well. Spending time to consider where you might experience problems and where you might find encouragement is smart planning. By reducing small obstacles and capitalizing on available facilitators, cultural change efforts can proceed more smoothly and result in greater success.

- *Planning for succession and future efforts by building memories and learning.* Every change effort has the potential to foster organizational learning and memories. While every effort cannot go smoothly, every effort has the potential to teach us things that worked (or didn't). In any case, smart school leaders consider the opportunities for learning and memory building, important aspects of the change effort. By attending to the process as well as the products of change, school cultures can be developed, enhanced, and sustained.

REFLECTIONS AND ACTIVITIES
FOR DEVELOPING SCHOOL CULTURE

Reflections

1. Consider the yin-yang diagram (Figure 4.1) of the management and leadership tasks.

   Look at your responses to the reflections activity from Chapter 2. If you did not complete this activity, do so now.

   What have you learned about diagnosis (Chapter 3) and leading cultural change (Chapter 4) that might influence where you allocate your time?

   Develop at least three or four specific leadership/management activities that would increase your ability to lead the cultural change process in your school.

2. Use the indicators of high and low PCOLT settings in Table 4.1 to reflect on your school setting.

   How widespread are each of these indicators in your school?

   Based on your reflection, what needs to change? How might you stimulate cultural changes?

Activities

Design a story for your school.

1. Choose the kind of story you wish to tell.
2. Clarify your purpose for telling the story by setting a clear goal you wish the story would help you to achieve.
3. Identify who will be the key players in your story.

   Name who you wish to recognize or what exemplifies the actions/challenges/values you wish to highlight.

4. Develop the narrative.

   What are the key events and actions you want to talk about?

   Under what circumstances did they occur?

   What challenges were faced?

   How were they overcome?

   Add an element of interest or surprise; make the story worth listening to.

5. Clarify specific outcomes.

What happened?

How does this story serve to illustrate your cultural challenge or change?

6. Try your story out on a few trusted colleagues and solicit feedback.

What was their reaction?

How did they respond?

What points might you sharpen, drop, or expand?

Did they clearly link the point of the story to the goals you wish the story to achieve?

7. Practice your story.

Be able to tell it smoothly and clearly.

Be able to use it to send a consistent message.

8. Deliberately choose how and when you will tell your story.

Think about where the story fits into your daily work.

Plan how you will work it into your conversation with your school community members.

Consider how you might make the story part of your school culture.

ANALYZING YOUR SCHOOL

Assessing Your Leadership Challenges

Leadership challenges come from the internal situation and the external environment. Assess your school and reflect on where your sources of challenge lie.

Situational Pressures (5 = Strongly disagree → 1 = Strongly agree)					
1. Our school is well positioned to be successful in the current environment.	5	4	3	2	1
2. Our school has an excellent reputation in the community.	5	4	3	2	1
3. The structure and behavior of key parent groups is stable and supportive.	5	4	3	2	1
4. Our district's policies are consistent and clear.	5	4	3	2	1
5. Our test scores are good and definitely not declining.	5	4	3	2	1
6. We are not undergoing any major changes that have created concerns or disruptions inside the school.	5	4	3	2	1
7. Teachers' skills are keeping pace with new research and demands.	5	4	3	2	1
8. New state curricular and testing changes are not likely to be difficult for us to implement.	5	4	3	2	1
9. Our student population is stable and we do not anticipate any significant changes.	5	4	3	2	1
10. We are not concerned about losing students to private schools or other schools of choice.	5	4	3	2	1
11. Our families are completely satisfied with the quality of the school.	5	4	3	2	1
12. Our district's taxpayers are satisfied with our costs and the value that they see.	5	4	3	2	1
13. We don't have a problem getting the resources that we need to do the job.	5	4	3	2	1
14. We don't need to worry about political or economic shifts affecting us significantly.	5	4	3	2	1
15. Well-qualified professionals are eager to fill all our job openings.	5	4	3	2	1
16. Labor relations are excellent in our school.	5	4	3	2	1

Add up the total for the sixteen items above. Your score could range from 16 to 80.

Interpreting Your Score

A score of 25 or lower indicates a fairly stable environment. A steady-as-she-goes strategy (continuous improvement focus) should be sufficient.

A score of 35 or above indicates a unstable environment. Expect precipitating events in such an environment, even though you cannot always predict what they will be or when they will occur. Be a flexible change master.

Above 60? You are in a pressure-cooker environment that demands a continuous change leadership focus.

Assessing the State of PCOLT in Your School

Where does your school stand when it comes to the PCOLT indicators?

Reflect on your school's culture by considering each indicator.

Rank those items in which is the indicator is strongly present a 3, those where the indicator is sporadically present a 2, and those where the indicator is weak a 1.

Which areas need attention? Which require continued nurturing? Do all school members agree? Where are the substantive areas of disagreement? How might those be addressed? What might be a primary area of focus for your school culture change efforts?

In my school . . .			
	3	2	1
Collective identity is present. We . . .			
Share a common focus for expectations and goals.			
Share norms and values about practice.			
Work together to address problems of practice.			
Discuss our learning with others and learn from others' efforts.			
A focus on learning is present. We . . .			
Regularly observe each other teach.			
Share memories that assist in new learning and change.			
Individually create new areas of expertise.			
Share what we know to help students learn, achieve, and succeed.			
Share measures of progress with each other and support each other in understanding what they mean.			
A philosophy of contribution is present. We . . .			
Share leadership roles and expectations.			
Participate in decision making.			
Relentlessly focus on teaching and learning goals.			
Trust is present. We . . .			
Cooperate and collaborate.			
Hold a strong communal identity.			
Openly, regularly, and reflectively discuss core issues of school improvement.			
Engage the external community in our school improvement efforts.			

5

Networks, Networking, And Culture Change

In the previous chapters, we introduced actions that you could take to improve culture and create intensified leadership in your building. If we stopped there we would leave you with the impression that the responsibility for creating culture change resides primarily with you and your administrative team. This is not, however, the whole picture. You need your own support network in order to do this work. In this chapter we draw on data from efforts to create effective principal networks in the United States, England, and Sweden, arguing that principals must become embedded in their own professional learning communities in order to stimulate reflective practice more effectively within their own school.[*]

In this chapter you will learn:

- why belonging to networks is important;
- how networks operate to support the culture change process in education and other sectors;
- how to get others involved in productive networks; and
- why, under some circumstances, networking and networks can detract from culture change.

---

[*]This chapter draws heavily on material provided by Lorna Earl (Aporia Consulting, Ltd.), David Jackson (former director of the Networked Learning Communities at the National College for School Leadership in England), and Hans-Åke Scherp (University of Karlstad, Sweden). The Networked Learning Communities Programme is a National College for School Leadership initiative.

WEBS AND NETS

We contend, based on our experience and the experiences of principals that we have worked with, that belonging to a network will sustain and support you as you move forward is important. A great deal of research substantiates the claim that membership in a group whose purpose is to foster action for school improvement will make a real difference in your capacity to lead and manage culture. Teachers need PCOLT to encourage experimentation and changed instruction; principals and other school leaders are no different in wanting access to fresh ideas and a low-risk environment in which to share their own practice. In particular, your web of relationships with other principals and stakeholders will have a critical impact on your ability to act as a transformational leader, focusing it on principles of quality and continuous improvement.

As a school leader, you already know in your bones that you are part of a complicated web of relationships that affects how you carry out your work. This is not unique to the decentralized educational system of the United States. One of our Danish colleagues, Leif Moos, created the image of the principal's job as part of a large spiderweb—an image that we find provocative and reproduce in Figure 5.1. Each of the boxes in the figure represents a group or an individual that is part of the leadership web; all exert influence over the outcomes of actions taken in a school. As we discussed in Chapter 4, the groups and individuals that are most influential will vary depending on the decision context: The mix of interested actors involved in discussions about raising a local school tax levy will not be the same as those who want to become involved in encouraging children to read more outside of school.

The lighter colored boxes in Figure 5.1 represent groups that have a legitimate stake in what goes on inside your school every day, while the darker boxes are those whose interest is also considerable, but less involved in the details. These groups are often seen as challenges for principals—sources of interference that must be managed through a delicate and often choreographed political dance. Surveys of principals suggest that they may represent interactions and tasks that are among your least preferred (Goldring & Hausman, 2001). Nevertheless, they are important to effective cultural leadership.

Viewing schools as webs of influence changes how we think about school operations because the image confronts our basic assumptions about orderliness and power (Spillane, Halverson, & Diamond, 2001). Principals are less middle managers in a bureaucratic pyramid (though it certainly feels that way at times) than activists in linking the contributions of many participants to the benefit of the school. While they have authority to act in some circumstances, most of what principals do is conditioned by the presence and influence of the many other stakeholders. In other words, as we argue in Chapter 4, they are the weavers of the cultural story.

Figure 5.1   Leadership Web

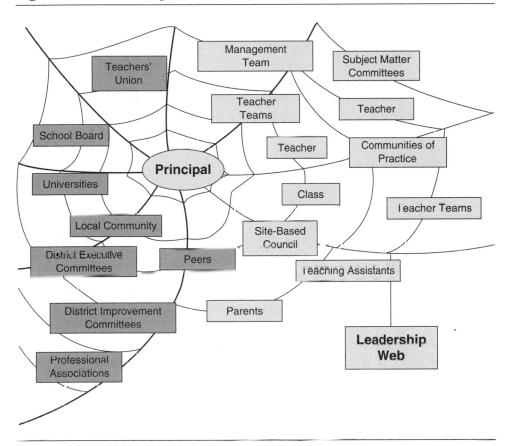

SOURCE: Adapted from Leif Moos, Danish University of Education.

What does it mean to think about schools as webs of influence rather than pyramids of authority? Most important, from our perspective, it means that creating good school cultures must be concerned less with re-arranging the formal structures within the school and increasingly with nimble decisions about who should be at the table when ideas are being debated and discussed. In addition, it means that you can broaden your thinking about who might be a source of support, and stop thinking about yourself and the other administrators in your building as an isolated team.

Nearly twenty years ago, two management scholars observed that, in "the variety of expectations, demands, needs, activities and approaches (that occur in schools), . . . [r]elationships that strike casual observers as haphazard and senseless appear regular and sensible when viewed from the perspective of those who must try to make sense out of all of the pieces" (Shedd & Bacharach, 1990, p. 191). Principals are not solely respon-sible for weaving a web of productive relationships among stakeholders, who range from individual teachers to professional associations that set standards, but they are increasingly expected to keep track of the status of the web. This means mending holes (when there are important gaps in communication and understanding among partners) and creaking links— and we will say more about this later.

Of course the image of the spider's web conjures up an additional fear that many leaders bring to work with them on a daily basis: How to avoid getting trapped in a sticky net of obligations, politics, back scratching, and inferred promises that can't be fulfilled? The unfortunate answer is that you can't; webs and nets are sticky and tough, and they can be traps for the unwary. But you can't change them back into neat bureaucracies by wishing that life were simpler.

THINKING ABOUT NETWORKS— WHY SHOULD WE CARE?

Manuel Castells argues that we are in the midst of revolutionary social change, from industrial and place-based forms of social organization to information-based and media-connected models (Castells, 2000). While this change resonates with schools' need to struggle with the vast content of the Internet and increasingly interactive learning styles, education changes slowly. No one expects that our brick-and-mortar schools will be replaced with modems and student-designed curricula in the near future, but we are all increasingly affected by the increased demands for communication and information.

So where do networks come in? First, *creating connections among people with similar interests and positions is easier*. Asking for advice about a problem of school leadership meant, in the very recent past, finding a colleague's phone number, hoping that the message would get delivered, and playing endless "phone tag" or fruitlessly searching for a time to meet. Today, a simple e-mail to a Listserv or a posting on a blog can get lots of input fast—even from strangers.

Second, *finding expertise is much simpler*. Think of what it used to take to get information about an issue like providing effective feedback to a struggling teacher. If you were lucky and had a competent professor for a human-resources course who was still in place, you might call him or her, but if the professor had retired or left, you might not know whom to call— and maybe the person had never handled this type of problem anyway. If you typed "feedback teacher supervision" into Google, you would be rewarded with more than 35,000 hits, and while it would take you a bit of time to look at them, even a half-hour spent perusing the first few pages would give you a list of strategies to consider.

Third, *proximity is no longer a limitation*. If you are a high-school principal in a district that has only one high school, finding local peers to talk to about critical issues isn't easy. But if you are in rural Nebraska, the chances are just as high that your best insights may come from a rural school in Oregon than the district twenty miles down the road. There is a new kind of space, according to Castells, the "space of flows" that is made up both of information systems and real people in real places. It may be more important that your electronically connected peers are in districts with recent and rapid increases in immigration than that they are located in a cold or warm climate, or in a "red" or "blue" state.

Fourth, *new perspectives are inevitable.* People who work in the same school or district inevitably come to accept the situation that they find themselves in. In the best case, a stable setting may provide you with all of the stimulation and new ideas that you need: your district and peers may be well connected, you may have good contacts with a local university, and the central office may have a wealth of expertise. If your situation is less optimal, on the other hand, you may find yourself in a collective "boiled frog" syndrome: The water has become hotter and hotter but, because you get used to it, you don't leap for other alternatives. Peter Senge (1990) writes compellingly about how the boiled frog syndrome holds organizations back. If you are part of a larger network, others can easily see alternatives and give you insights about your system that may help you to push for improvement.

Networks, Learning, and Change

More important than any of the four practical issues listed above is the fact that organizing an adaptive, learning school requires that school leaders become networked. Research on both individual and group learning suggests that powerful learning environments require "weak ties" rather than strong connections (Granovetter, 1973). Inventions in practice and other new ideas usually enter a person or school's consciousness because another person with whom they are only loosely connected introduces them. Your best friends and closest colleagues already know most of what you know—and vice versa. Though they may help you work through the details of "how to do it" because of their intimate knowledge of your setting, they are less likely to have to provide you with a genuinely new idea than someone you know less well. And if you only talk to the people you know best, you are less likely to change. As David Jackson noted in a 2006 presentation, "You can't have professional learning communities without permeability to external learning—otherwise all you do is recycle the existing knowledge-base." We know that innovations in practice diffuse more broadly through social networks that link individuals, and that people and organizations that are not linked with others tend to be more resistant to change (Abrahamson & Rosenkopf, 1997). We also know that electronic networks are helping people to solve problems that they can't resolve on their own or with local knowledge (Constant, Sproull, & Kiesler, 1996).

What is true for individuals is also true for organizations, both public and private. In business, increasing attention is being paid to the importance of strategic alliances among firms that are also competitors— not to constrain "the market" but because they promote genuinely new products and processes and further the firms' individual interests. For example, a study of biotechnology firms concludes that "the locus of innovation will be found in networks of learning, rather than in individual firms. The large-scale reliance on interorganizational collaborations in the biotechnology industry reflects a fundamental and pervasive concern with access to knowledge" (Powell, Koput, & Smith-Doerr, 1996, p. 132). The same is true for organizations in the public sector, where isolation tends to reduce effectiveness both in achieving service goals and in maintaining internal vitality.

Many school leaders (and teachers) think that creating a successful school is a zero-sum game: If one school does well, it attracts "good" students from a neighboring school—they look better and we look less good. The data suggest, however, that this competitive "antinetwork" mentality is a predictor of decline rather than success.

David Jackson emphasizes the need for both within school ties (professional learning communities) and external ties (networked learning communities) to create change. Just as the web shown in Figure 5.1 distinguishes between lighter (internal) and darker (external) stakeholders, he points out that both are essential components of a change model that acknowledges the importance of collective, collaborative work. Jackson's depiction of the relationship is shown in Figure 5.2.

Partly as a consequence of this robust research base, much effort in the United States has gone into developing teacher networks as a part of efforts to revitalize professional development and to improve classroom practice, with significant results (Lieberman, 2000). In contrast, limited attention has been paid to the development of networks among principals. Both of the authors of this book have helped to organize and support principal networks in our local areas, and we observe that at first principals feel that coming to meetings to talk to each other is an indulgence— instead of having coffee and doughnuts at 7 AM, they should be at school, sorting out the anticipated problems of the day and going over attendance questions. But principals come to understand that rather than wasting time, they are saving time by finding common solutions to common problems, by organizing a coherent position on what schools need to implement a new district or state agenda, and figuring out how to manage difficult problems, such as introducing a new teacher supervision model that is neither district nor union approved.

Figure 5.2   Professional Learning Communities/Networked Learning Communities

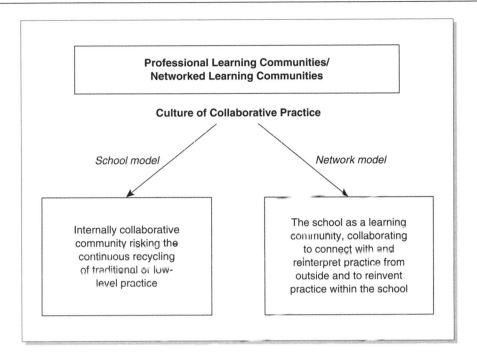

SOURCE: D. Jackson. (2006). *From PLCs to NLCs.* Paper presented at the International Congress for School Effectiveness and School Improvement, Barcelona, Spain.

HOW DO YOU KNOW WHAT TO DO NEXT?

Richard Elmore, a political scientist who has spent most of his career thinking about large educational policy issues, has long argued that the most important ability for principals is knowing the right thing to do. As Elmore notes in his descriptions of the principal collaborative that he has organized in Cambridge, Massachusetts, he has come to believe that participation in semipermanent networks is what keeps them vital and focused. Rather than principals being part of a loose set of unpredictable relationships from which they can glean new ideas, the point of formal networks is to give school leaders the certainty that they have a safe place to connect with peers—and with university researchers who may provide "loose ties" to emerging knowledge to foster more reflection (see Elmore, 2000, 2005).

Look around in your school. The teachers who are the most vital, the most up to date, and the most influential are very likely those who engage in professional dialogue outside the school as well as inside. While professional community inside is important, it is rarely sufficient to develop a strong reflective culture. We know from studies of learning in networks that teachers' discourse was stronger and more "significant" for learning when they talked with others from different settings and backgrounds. While this can happen in a single episode, it is most likely to occur in more stable groups in which teachers participate for a longer period of time and feel like members (Wilson & Berne, 1999).

All of this is may sound rather abstract if you are not already part of a professional network—in other words, if the networks between you, your peers, and other stakeholders are disconnected or difficult to understand. But wait a minute—you probably are in more networks that you think! For example, if you have been going to your state professional association meetings for more than a few years, you've probably already connected with some people with whom you feel a shared understanding of the emotional and technical content of the work of shaping schools. You may not see them between meetings, but you connect when you see each other. Or, if you are in a larger district or an urban area, there may be other professional associations that bring you into contact with people whom you see as allies and even professional friends. When you are in a productive network—one in which ideas about improvement outweigh complaints about pressure— don't you come back to your own work refreshed and enlivened?

Networks—Self-Organizing or Organized?

There is disagreement about how networks can best be organized. On the one hand, there are idealists, largely following the "communities of practice" literature popularized by Etienne Wenger (1998), that argue that they are distinctively organic and should arise from natural affinities that draw people together around shared problems. They mimic natural communities in which people seek out others—in churches, social groups, and otherwise—whose problems or issues make them "like us." In this sense, they are they opposite of "teams" that are identified by the organization as having responsibility for improving organizationally defined processes and products. Team goals are often explicit and membership is clear.

In schools, the contrast would be between the group of professionals who informally—during lunch or before and after school—discuss how to improve ninth-grade transitions (as we saw in Metro High School in Chapter 2) and the professional team that is designated by the principal to design and staff a ninth-grade academy. In the best of all possible worlds, they may be one and the same—but often they are not. Metro's informal group was bound by values or convictions, by trust, and by a sense of connection around a topic—better assignments that integrated two subject areas—that made them passionate. The ninth-grade teams that we have studied are comprised of those who teach or advise ninth graders—often the newest faculty, since many high-school teachers prefer older students (Louis & Freeman, 2007).

For principals, the difference would be between a small group of principals who choose to "comentor" because they have similar school settings, and a larger group, convened by the district, for the explicit purpose of creating dynamic learning environments. As described by Jackson, principal networks of the latter type focus on:

- Joint work groups (e.g., project teams, curriculum development groups)
- Collective planning (e.g., steering groups, professional development groups)
- Mutual problem-solving teams (e.g., focus groups)
- Collaborative inquiry groups (e.g., inquiry teams)
- Shared professional development activities (learning forums/joint staff days) (Jackson, 2006)

But there is evidence that this distinction between the naturally occurring affinity group and the formal team is less important in practice than in theory. Teacher networks do not have to be spontaneous, or teacher-initiated and run, in order to be successful; state or district sponsored networks can also successfully increase learning, motivation, and empowerment (Firestone & Pennell, 1997; Kruse & Louis, 2007). This is also true for principals. Two key examples of successful networking efforts for principals are from England and Sweden.

NETWORKED LEARNING COMMUNITIES

The National College for School Leadership and the government sponsored a major project to link 1,000 schools into smaller groups whose purpose was to share ideas and to work on solving common problems. The project linked the clusters of schools with other agencies, including local districts, universities, and consultants. As one of those with responsibility for overseeing the networks commented, "Networked Learning Communities are purposefully led social entities that are characterised by a commitment to quality, rigour and a focus on outcomes. . . . They promote the dissemination of good practice; enhance the professional development of teachers, support capacity building in schools. They also mediate between centralised and decentralised structures, and assist in the process of re-structuring and re-culturing educational organisational systems" (Jackson, 2006). In other words, the networks not only were places where ideas could be shared, but also represented an effort to create more intellectual energy for reform at the grassroots level.

Two Canadians, Lorna Earl and Steven Katz, carried out an assessment of the implementation and impact of the networks using both surveys and interviews with leaders in twenty schools (Earl & Katz, 2008). The results were clear: involvement by the principal in a formal network had a significant association with student achievement outcomes in both reading and mathematics, and had an even stronger effect on improved teaching practices. Since the lag between change in practice and changes in standardized student achievement scores is well known, the long-term impacts of leadership participation on student learning are probably understated by their findings.

From our perspective, one of the most encouraging results was that participation in a network increased principals' efforts to intensify leadership. Being involved in supportive groups gave many principals the courage to let go of their sense that they were solely responsible for coming up with solutions for school problems. Some representative quotes from Earl and Katz (2008):

> One of the meetings where we were looking at distributed leadership and how we could empower coordinators, it suddenly made me realize I had not taken it on board. And I don't think the other head teachers had any strategies either. I realized these coordinators were going to meetings and I hadn't taken the time to sit down with them and discuss needs and how could what you've learned be used better in school. (p. 240)

> I know people say leadership from the middle, but actually I'm not even sure middle is right anymore. I mean I look to (paraprofessional classroom aides) at times, and I think of really great skill there, and encourage that. . . . I have got the opportunity to encourage that (from the network). (p. 241)

The authors conclude that the culture of leadership had changed to "sharing without controlling" in the twenty schools that they visited, a conclusion backed up by the larger survey.

NETWORKED LEARNING GROUP—SWEDEN

The networked learning communities developed in Sweden are based on the belief that learning occurs in groups and around common problems. The main idea of problem-based school development is "to find better ways to handle everyday problems, teachers and school leaders deepen their understanding of the nature of the problems in learning groups." The project has organized over 1,200 teachers in PBL networks, over 400 school leaders in two regional networks. A major focus of the networks is examining problems of practice, reflecting on them, and transcribing collective understandings in minutes that are available to all members of the networks. School leader PBL work focuses on broad issues related to school development and the promotion of school improvement. The network is supported through regular voluntary meetings for both larger and smaller groups.

Teachers who participated in the networks along with their principals were particularly enthusiastic about the way in which involvement in the networks has changed the level of discourse between teachers and principals over pedagogical issues (Scherp & Scherp, 2007).

Both district and school leaders' response to the networks has been overwhelming positive. Hans-Åke Scherp, who initiated the project, recently commented, "Last week we had a meeting with ten communities that have been in the network for five years. All of them wanted to prolong their participation, which tells us that it is perceived as a very important means to support school development" (Scherp, personal communication, 2007). A recent survey of participants indicated that principals are very positive about the extent to which the network meetings contribute to a deeper understanding of their school's development processes, and value in particular its significance in keeping them in touch with other schools and communities in helping relationships. Scherp goes on to say, "The school leaders have, to a greater extent, become leaders of the learning processes among teachers compared to more traditional leadership where their main task is to organize and plan the teachers' activities" (Scherp, personal communication, 2007).

Networks and Intellectual Leadership

What tools will principals gain from being part of a larger network outside of the district or area in which his or her school is located? We know from research that principals are most effective when they act as "intellectual leaders" within their schools. Well-regarded educational leadership scholars assert that intellectual leadership is at the core of the changing demands on principals (Murphy, 2002; Sergiovanni, 1998). Ken Leithwood and his colleagues (Leithwood, Jantzi, & Steinbach, 1998) show that intellectual leadership is one of the transformational practices that allow leaders to have an impact on classroom practice.

At the same time, the power of principals to screen information that contributes to collective discussion and reflection in schools is also apparent. Principals set agendas for meetings (either formally or informally), often review the work of teacher professional development committees, and make decisions about what articles to stuff in teacher's mailboxes. Even schools that are well under way in implementing more broadly distributed or shared leadership models usually have principals who are both cheerleaders and gatekeepers for new ideas.

Recent research shows the impact of networking on teacher's views of their principal as an intellectual leader. The same surveys were administered to schools that were part of an action-research project that was not connected with networking support and those involved in the problem-based network described above. In the networked schools, over 75 percent of the principals were regarded as active intellectual participants in discussions about school improvement and pedagogy, contrasted with approximately 50 percent in the nonnetworked schools. Even more impressive, in the networked schools, 30 percent of the teachers identified dialogue with their principal as a major influence on their classroom practice—as contrasted with 10 percent of the teachers in a project with similar goals, but without the support of networks (Scherp, personal communication, 2007).

Lorna Earl and Steven Katz also conclude that access to external expertise—not only the collective experiences of other principals, but also a network facilitators, who were often engaged scholars from universities—increased the ability of the participants to be effective intellectual leaders within their staff. As they suggest, the big change that comes from network participation is to help leaders to understand their schools as places where people think about their work, as well as develop and apply knowledge (Earl & Katz, 2006).

In sum, there is powerful evidence that networks are highly effective at facilitating culture change, moving schools in the direction of becoming learning organizations, and creative more effective collaborative leadership in which the principal is seen as a transformational intellectual leader.

CAUTIONS

Networks are not a "magic bullet" that will meet all of the needs that principals and others encounter in their work. Unless there is unbiased availability of experts (both practitioner-experts and scholars), networks can result in the rapid diffusion of bad ideas—or bad strategies for implementation of good ideas. Networks can, without external support from a university or a principal center, erode very quickly under the pressures to "mind the store" back at the school, leaving participants disillusioned about the return on their investment of time and enthusiasm. Earl and Katz's (2008) report, for example, that some participants in networks found that the extra work involved in participating was a burden—the idea was applauded, but the energy just wasn't there. Similarly, principals and schools who become active in networks are likely to be among the higher performing rather than the neediest schools; any advances that they make may widen disparities between schools rather than close them. This issue parallels studies of networks among parents, which suggest that no matter what districts do, higher income parents tend to have better information networks than lower income parents, and that parent networks exhibit a high degree of racial segregation (Schneider, Teske, Roch, & Marschall, 1997). Starting a network requires resources, external support, and firm mutual commitments to keep at the work and to develop a strong sense of mutual responsibility.

NEXT STEPS

But how is a busy principal to incorporate all of this responsibility for the intellectual life of his or her school into a schedule that is already crowded? And how, given the limited opportunities that principals have for sustained professional development, are they to gain access to the knowledge and connections to keep internal conversations alive? For most experienced school leaders, there is a sense that this is *not* what they signed on for when they began their licensure programs! The first step is to look for the resources around you that can build on resources that you already have. Here is a list of suggestions:

- *Build on what you already have.* If you already have a set of colleagues that you trust and feel compatible with, suggest that you meet more formally to discuss new ideas and problems of practice. Just make sure that there is a clear agenda and "real work" so that your time together doesn't become a gripe session!
- *See what the district might do.* Most districts have become aware that professional development opportunities for principals have lagged behind what is needed. If you work in a small district, ask the superintendent to find colleagues who might be interested in sponsoring a network; if you are in a large district, ask for funds to develop a professional community for administrators.
- *Turn to a local university.* If you have contacts with faculty members who are interested in school improvement, the chances are that they already will have begun to be interested in networking and professional communities. Perhaps they would be willing to act as a facilitator in getting a group started, finding a place to meet, and making contacts with other researchers who might be interested in engaging with your group.
- *Turn to your state professional association.* Most professional associations are also becoming aware of the importance of networking, and may be able to find grant funds to foster networks, either virtual or physical, that extend beyond the usual meetings.
- *Find a virtual community.* We can make no recommendations about this because the reality of the Web is that it is ever changing. We do know that finding these networks is not simple, and we hope that they will grow rapidly in the future.

The overall message of this chapter has been straightforward, in part because the base of experience with principal networks is, compared to the previous chapters, thin. The major points are, therefore, rather clear:

1. You are inevitably part of a network of groups and organizations that you influence and that influence you.

2. What you probably lack is a strong network that can support you in your professional development, and that can provide strategic and short-term help as you confront problems in developing your school's culture and intensifying leadership.

3. Given a policy context that increasingly presses for simple bench-marks and assumes that leaders can "control" learning outcomes, a support network is important to sustaining your emotional and intellectual energy.

4. You can work on these issues with colleagues in your school, but you will find that your outlook and success "at home" will be enhanced by sustained connections with peers who are struggling with similar decision contexts and pressures.

In sum, as you turn away from quick fixes toward long-term success, par-ticipating in (or even starting) a network can help you face the increasingly hard work of school leadership if your group maintains a focus on school improvement and problem solving.

REFLECTIONS AND GOAL-SETTING ACTIVITIES

A Reflection

Create your own leadership web. Figure 5.3 illustrates the potential groups that are part of your leadership environment. Using this web as a starting point, draw a web that identifies the supportive resources avail-able to you.

1. Which do you use most often? Least often? Why?

2. How might you work to tap the resources available to you in more productive ways?

3. Identify groups or individuals in your web that may inhibit your leadership. How can you develop relationships with other network members that may minimize their effects on you?

Figure 5.3   Kruse-Louis Web

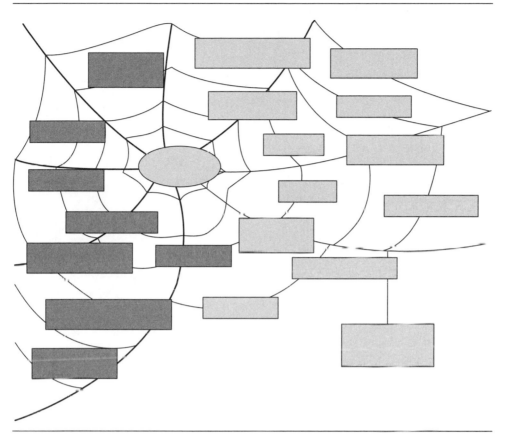

Set Networking Goals

1. Networks offer their members two important resources—support and information. We encourage you to go to more conferences to develop a network of your own. The national associations have chapters in most states, but there are also many specialized conferences that may be more appropriate, ranging from specialized programs such as High Schools That Work, to state agency conferences on specialized topics. You should set yourself a goal of going to at least one new conference a year.

2. Invite three to five other principals you know to join an in-person or online network.

   Find someone who can help facilitate the group. If at all possible, this person should be "neutral" (a university faculty member or a sympathetic administrator from your district).

Set explicit goals for becoming a supportive learning community and a commitment to meet.

Develop a variety of topics for discussion and solicit ideas from other principals.

Meet at least once a month and treat the meetings as "sacred time."

6

Intensifying Leadership Through Partnerships With Districts

Schools are not autonomous—they are positioned in districts that provide a legal, policy, and resource context that deeply affects the work of schools. Whether your school is located in a small town or an urban center, the case materials presented in this chapter will suggest ways in which you can work more effectively with your district as a partner. Working well with districts is not the same as being compliant. School leaders must work within *and* challenge district policy and practice in order to contribute effectively to comprehensive student achievement. As we shall see later in this chapter, the development of closer relationships between schools and districts is deeply linked to the arguments that we made for networks as a foundation for

---

In this chapter you will learn:

- why working to create voice for the common good of students is important;
- how to find allies and partners for school improvement efforts;
- why becoming an effective "outlaw" when temporary toxicity strikes a district can foster positive results; and
- how to work within a system where ineffective leadership is present.

improved school cultures and intensified leadership. Skillfully developed, they can assist you in intensifying leadership and changing school culture.

THINKING ABOUT DISTRICT-SCHOOL RELATIONSHIPS

Our work with building and district leaders suggests that in many cases the relationship is, at best, tense. Building principals often feel overwhelmed by the amount of work that district office personnel expect them to accomplish. District leaders often wonder how principals spend their days when there is no clear increase in student test scores. We see how each of these observations is, at least in part, reasonable. As we argued in Chapter 2, school leaders may find themselves mired in the daily management tasks of the school (many of which they see as promulgated by the district) and have little time on the substantive issues of leadership. As Tony Bryk and his colleagues observe, district leaders often shower schools with uncoordinated innovations, adoptions, and programs, hanging each on already overburdened improvement agendas like ornaments on a Christmas tree (Bryk, Sebring, Kerbow, Rollow, & Easton, 1998). Furthermore, when so many initiatives and priorities are unclear, it is no wonder principals often can't make sense of all they are expected to accomplish. From the district's perspective, principals have not always lived up to their obligations as instructional leaders, and in an era in which all schools are being held to the same standards, variability among schools is a problem for districts.

A study of New York City's innovative District 2 suggests that district personnel saw disparity in school performance as largely attributable to the ability of the principal to deal with the unique circumstances of their school. The district's job was to nudge, control, and negotiate, depending on how the principal responded to new pressures for performance (Elmore & Burney, 1998). In practice, however, district time to support principals was also limited, and there was a de facto categorization of principals and schools into four categories: (1) "free agents" who were with the district program and doing well; (2) "with-the-drill" newish principals who needed some support but could be trusted; (3) "watch list" schools, with principals deemed to be capable, but with low performance; and (4) "off-the-screen" schools, where the schools were not perceived as engaged in improvement, but the district simply had no clear plan. The point of the categorization was that it guided district staff in the provision of their limited attention—support tended to go to with-the-drill schools and narrower oversight to watch-list schools. Neither free agents or off-the-screen schools got much systematic attention. Schools also reported differential access to support and attention.

So, what is the underlying school-district problem? Everyone agrees that:

- *All schools are different.* They have different student populations, different teachers, and different resources, even when the district-allocated budget is equitable.

- *All schools are supposed to be equally good*, but there are no clear guideposts for what that means, aside from state tests.

No wonder that the relationships between principals and district staff are, more frequently than not, fraught with tension. You understand the importance of standards and a core curriculum and assessment practices, and you know what your school needs in order to make these work. However, when district initiatives are insensitive to differences among schools, they do not lead to organizational learning and trust. Evidence suggests that when relationships between the district and the school are clearly defined and explicit, when responsibility for student learning is shared across all levels of the school district, and when policy and practice within the district are aligned, the potential for student success is increased (Desimone, Porter, Birman, Garet, & Yoon, 2002; Schmoker, 1999). The following case offers an example of a successful district-school partnership.

FOCUSING ON STUDENT LEARNING AS A COMMON GOOD

Both teachers and the community consider the Spencer city schools excellent. With a long-standing focus on innovation, Spencer initially responded to state accountability initiatives by providing new reading and math programs during daylong in-service sessions with follow-up training. However, as the state's benchmarks increasingly focused on individual achievement gains, the district shifted its approach. The superintendent and curriculum director had previously emphasized *what and how* teachers taught, but now shifted to stress the role of teachers in assessing how well students were *learning* the material. Moreover, learning for all became the district's hallmark: it was no longer acceptable for only some students to demonstrate high performance.

The superintendent and curriculum director began by holding daylong meetings of teachers and school leaders to deepen their understanding of the state's standards and to initiate discussions about how formative classroom assessment influenced instructional and curricular decisions. Rather than considering each grade level or subject area as distinct, they began to ask how the curriculum and instruction provided within the district added up to a coherent educational whole. With district support (and a little pressure) clear shifts occurred in conversations at the school level. Across the district, dialogue about instruction and assessment decisions increasingly focused on how the curriculum could provide students the skills and knowledge necessary to become successful adults. The shift was more than cosmetic; teachers began to see the way in which instructional choices in their classrooms played a part in overall outcomes for students.

The Spencer schools story ends with two positive outcomes. The first was predictable. They are the leading district in the state for individual student achievement gains as well as federally required schoolwide yearly progress results. The second was more surprising. Teachers report a greater sense of connection with each other and interest in collaborating, including efforts that cross grade and subject area boundaries.

The experience of the Spencer city schools suggests that improvements in culture can occur when districts get their act together, but on the surface it appears that the role of the principal as an instructional leader has been bypassed. As we shall see below, however, this was not the case.

RETHINKING ORGANIZATIONAL STRUCTURES AND CULTURE

Spencer schools succeeded because they were willing to redefine and to rethink the district organization. By creating guided opportunities for teachers and school leaders to learn together, district leaders could change the relationship between teachers and principals. These changes included shifts in the ways both principals and teachers worked. For principals, this meant increased responsibility for classroom practice, including understanding new instructional and assessment tools. By shifting from a traditional focus on "my kids, this year" to "our kids, across their school careers," teachers began to understand the power of working more closely with their colleagues, including the principal. No longer was the conversation about simply reading or math, freshman and juniors; it was about implementing practices designed to foster increased student learning within subjects and across grade levels.

On the surface this appears simple. It is not. It required that everyone in the district rethink the core purpose of their daily tasks. The effort is an example of how intensifying leadership efforts across the district can shape school culture. Because everyone—including building and district personnel—was part of the improvement effort, things changed in the district office and in all schools. Leadership was symbolic, because teachers were able to observe district and school leaders learning and participating side by side with them, rather than telling them what to do. Principals also felt empowered by the effort, and believed that the district (and their teachers) expected them to play a significant role in shaping how the new emphasis evolved in their buildings.

The number of people able (and willing) to lead improvement efforts in schools expanded, as did the number of teachers and principals who could lead smaller grade level or subject area efforts.

In many ways, the Spencer example offers us a vision of best practice. We realize that things do not always go so easily. Established leaders may not believe they need to get in line with new policy and practice. Trust, either due to past transgressions or the presence of new leadership, may be absent, and principals may need to have strategies for "managing" their relationships with districts rather than expecting instant collaboration.

Growing Allies From Within—From the District and School Perspective

There are real organizational boundaries between schools and districts. Membership is clear to almost everyone: paychecks may come from the district, but teachers, students, and parents feel a sense of "belonging" to a school. It has long been observed that the links between districts and schools are loose rather than tight. Despite an on-paper hierarchy of authority, school systems operate more like franchises, in which stores are locally owned within a set of more or less clear guidelines. This observation reflects, of course, the fundamental value tension articulated above: "We're all different" and "We should all perform equally well using the same benchmarks." But boundaries aside, principals are increasingly connected in an age of accountability where districts are also held responsible for results delivered by their schools. So, if they are linked at the hip but have difficulty managing connection, how can they work together more profitably?

One answer, as we will see below, lies in the ability to manage highly personal relationships. District-school alliances are rarely about rules and rights (except when politicians get involved), but about how people talk to each other and the temporary agreements they come to.

RIDGE SCHOOL DISTRICT AND THE RESIDENT CURMUDGEON

When Superintendent Susan Bellows arrived at Ridge School District, the principal of the high school presented her with a challenge. A fifteen-year veteran of the district, Kevin Marin barely tolerated administrative council meetings. His past experience with previous superintendents suggested that valuable time was best invested at the building level, and his strategy (which had worked in the past) was to minimize his involvement at the district level and hope that strong performance would insulate him from unwelcome interference. On good days, he returned district e-mail on his BlackBerry, but he avoided in-person meetings.

Bellows worked to draw in Marin. She asked for his opinion and demonstrated that she valued it. She took notes when he spoke, probing him for district traditions and history. When an opportunity to appoint new leadership for the strategic planning committee arose, Bellows asked for his help. She came to his building and took time to talk with him about why he became a principal and what he hoped his legacy might be. Over a period of two years, he became more vocal, offering opinions and observations on the district. He began to attend district workshops and in-services. As his attitude changed, Bellows pushed and prodded, eliciting even greater involvement and commitment. In turn, his support for Bellows and her school improvement agenda grew.

This case illustrates how gradual interpersonal overtures can heal divisions that developed over a long period. This, of course, is not always successful; some people are so set in their ways that they cannot be moved (and must be moved around or moved out). But the example goes both ways. Principals also need to develop personal relationships with district administrators, who are used to dealing with the curmudgeons and don't know how to react to a principal who is looking for partnership.

VALLEYFIELD HIGH, REDUX

The former principal, Ira Greene, was a close personal friend of the superintendent, but was also viewed as an obstacle to intensified leadership because of his insistence on tight personal control over the school. In this small town, under state pressure to improve, the superintendent saw the hiring of the new principal, Norma Shale, as an opportunity to quickly move the school in a different direction. During the first six months of Norma's tenure, visits from either an associate superintendent or the superintendent himself were frequent, and the associate superintendent often dropped in unannounced in teachers' classrooms. When he saw something that he didn't like (a drowsy or disengaged student), he would make his displeasure public and clear.

Norma, new to her job, was caught between the proverbial rock (the teachers' union, which was beginning to threaten grievances) and a hard place (pressure from the district). She was particularly concerned that the goodwill that most teachers felt toward her and her new plans for comprehensive change would be undermined by tensions over "administrative interference." Norma was at her wit's end because she felt that her first few months on the job were critical to creating a new school culture that focused on collaboration and teacher leadership.

Her strategy was simple: She first met privately with the superintendent and associate superintendent to discuss a basic agreement about the school's deficiencies and needed directions. She also mustered her new teacher-leadership team to do a presentation about implementation plans and benchmarks. Only when she felt that she had convinced the district staff that they could work together as a team did she broach the subject of how she wanted "drop-in" classroom observations to change. Because she was nonconfrontational, clear about performance objectives, and open-ended in her request for a change in close district supervision, she was allowed to proceed. Her collaboration with the "dragon from the central office" paid off both within the school and with the superintendent.

INFLUENCING DISTRICT-SCHOOL RELATIONSHIPS: ALLIANCES AS NETWORKS OF INFLUENCE

As our vignettes indicate, at times it is necessary for district leaders to build alliances within the ranks of building leadership. At other times, alliances need to be created from the school building up. As demonstrated in the Ridge and Valleyfield examples, such efforts take time, and when a new leader is hired, relationships, roles, and responsibilities are often unclear. Add to that the commonplace observation that deeply engrained habits are hard to change, and you begin to understand the difficulty leaders on both sides of the school/district divide face when they seek to confront a history of poor leadership and management. A cycle of resistance followed by increased oversight quickly becomes counterproductive. In order for poor and inconsistent practice within and across schools to be changed, the development of alliances is critical.

Alliances occur around mutual interests and cooperative activities; they are strengthened when progress is made toward shared goals. Even Machiavelli acknowledged that alliances are critical to the development of strong leadership, and he cautions, in particular, that leaders without allies are likely to be isolated and unable to gain organizational traction. In a modern, non-Machiavellian world, alliances are not merely strategic, they are also part of building trust in leadership.

They are also part of building networks of support for leadership and change. In the previous chapter we explored the importance of peer networks as part of developing your own professional community. Where districts entered the picture, they were often as sources of expert (outside) help. Building a network of allies involves understanding the story of reform not only from the inside out (your perspective as you try to get resources to do what you want) but also from the outside in (understanding what others want and need from you) (Fullan, 2000).

Ridge and Valleyfield districts both showed that the first step in creating allies involves building (or rebuilding) trust. In both cases, one party saw that they needed a different kind of relationship with someone on the other side of a school-district boundary, and reached out with an understanding of their position and needs. By choosing to be an "alliance-maker" they could transcend formal organizational borderlines and pathways, and in turn develop consensus around and support for common goals and efforts.

By identifying potential benefits of an alliance, a leader can engender support for purposes and directions, but new alliances are also important as a means of cementing older alliances as well. Some of the potential benefits of developing alliances include:

- *A broader and more diverse base of support.* When alliances are formed, they can expand the base of support for improvement initiatives. The broader a leader's foundation of support, the more likely they will be to attract other influential allies. Susan Bellows needed the high-school principal in order to encourage other principals that a district team might have real payoff, and Norma Shale needed the respect of the associate superintendent to gain breathing room as she worked on shaping a new culture at Valleyfield.

- *Greater reserves of leadership.* As leadership is diversified and intensified across and within schools, the pool from which support and energy can be drawn grows as well. Having a larger pool from which to draw assistance and collaboration can enhance the district's and school's ability to respond productively to new circumstances rather than flailing about for the next innovation. In Valleyfield, the associate superintendent may have been out of bounds in popping into teachers' classrooms and "ratting" on them, but he was extremely knowledgeable and well connected with resources around the state.

- *Opportunities for compensatory leadership.* As leaders, we all have strengths and weaknesses; joining forces with others increases overall capacity. When school and district leaders come together to solve the problems are practice, the resulting choices are more likely to "fit" and create shared cultural values. When Bellows and Marin began to work as allies in the Ridge district, together they were building bridges between the old and new.

- *Greater resilience in the face of adversity.* When the leadership knowledge and skill set are deepened through alliances, schools become better able to address problems. Valleyfield was under intense scrutiny because of its very poor student performance; having a strong alliance between the school and the district about the potential for the new comprehensive reform effort was invaluable in negotiating "wiggle room" with the state and the older teachers.

- *Greater range and intensity of connections.* Allies often come to the table with their own partners and associates. By developing allies in one area of the organization or community, leaders gain access to the resources and relationships of others. In turn, this increases the potential of the district and school to respond when necessary. Valleyfield's associate superintendent had come to the district with deep experience in high-poverty urban settings nearby. He has old connections that could help the "urbanlike" but isolated rural high school to supplement the professional development provided by the state.

Where Alliances Seem Impossible

Until now we have considered districts and schools characterized by productive or at least improving relationships. We are aware that this is not the case everywhere, and we turn now to considering how school leaders might thrive when they work in districts where conditions are less encouraging. We consider two distinct responses to this condition. The first involves activity resisting a negative culture; the second addresses working with ineffective district leadership.

OUTLAWS AND REBELS

After years of static performance and low morale, the staff at Dunlap Middle School felt they had finally turned a corner. The eighth-grade basketball team made the state finals, a long-promised renovation had been completed, and weak test scores were slowly improving. The principal, Elliott Preston, credited the change to the retirement of a half-dozen veterans and his ability to hire a cadre of new, energetic teachers. For the first time in years, Dunlap looked and felt "new." Unfortunately, its resurgence was poorly timed with events in the surrounding district. A levy had recently failed, the area's major employer had announced massive layoffs, and district achievement gains had stalled. As negativity across the district grew, Preston was unwilling to accept that his fate was tied to the larger organization. Instead, he focused on continuing to motivate and engage his staff, openly announcing that they would not fall prey to the district's malaise. Instead, he suggested that the staff turn a blind eye to that which "stood in the way of our progress." In a staff meeting, he asked teachers to celebrate the successes and called on the staff to become strong together and "withstand the negative forces that might bring us down."

At a district meeting, he and his staff arrived focused on the events of the day. When it became clear that the intended professional development work had been usurped by a discussion about the district's woes, they walked out en masse. Unwilling to become distracted from their accomplishments and loath to embrace the self-pity of those around them, the staff turned inward, supporting the positive elements of their work. They focused efforts on those goals they thought were possible and celebrated their successes. Intentionally, openly, and honestly they focused on building their school culture to protect themselves from the negative environment that surrounded them.

Temporary Toxicity

When negative circumstances arise, even the best of district environments can become temporarily toxic. Overwhelmed by the sheer weight of conflict or pressure to accomplish the impossible, leaders can lose focus and direction. Yet how you react is your choice. You can, in frustration, hop on the bandwagon of bitterness and bemoan your school's circumstance. Or you can realize that the students will keep coming to school every day, and they want to learn. Leaders who choose the latter will focus on creating resilient cultures that can withstand temporary bumps in the road. We have seen the following responses work effectively in a variety of schools.

- *Accept the circumstance and carefully frame your response.* You have the right to feel badly when things go wrong. However, successful leaders acknowledge the feeling, hold a short pity-party, and move on. By reframing the event (e.g., "the sky is falling" versus "these are difficult times—we have seen them before"), leaders can manage communication with the school, direct attention to the goals and ends that matter, and ultimately survive the storm.

- *Realistically assess the situation and anticipate the most essential problems.* Ask the question, "How are things? Really?" Knowing where you stand in real terms helps you to make sound and timely decisions. Think of the problem in terms of how it will affect a variety of stakeholders—parents, students, teachers, and the community. By standing in the shoes of each group, you will begin to identify the primary targets of your actions and respond accordingly.
- *Stay focused on what matters.* In the end, student learning and success are what matters. You don't have to be swept up in minor details and issues, and you can remind others who are distracted to keep the end in mind. Focusing on your purpose and vision will encourage staff to help each other to filter and shape the choices that are made.
- *Look toward the future.* Temporary toxicity really can be temporary. It lasts only if you allow the negative to invade your school cultures. Your ability to ride out the storm is, in part, influenced by how future-oriented you can be. By planning for better times, one helps create them.

Working Around Bad Leadership

When Americans are asked to think about what comes to mind when they hear the word *leadership*, their responses will be largely positive and suggest trust and confidence. But bad leadership is a fact of life, and something that most people have experienced. This condition is particularly difficult to manage because even if the tenure of a bad superordinate is relatively short, a great deal of damage can be done to individuals and to schools. When temporary toxicity due to finances or a poor relationship with the press is compounded by ineffective leadership in the district office or in other schools, the problems may be much greater.

A "DREAM JOB" OR A BAD DREAM?

After years in a small rural district, Michael Aleno was hired to lead a K–4 building in a well-established, affluent district. As the opening of school neared, he spent time learning about the building he was to lead. He offered teachers gift certificates to a local bookstore as incentive for dropping by so that he might meet each one individually. He hosted an ice-cream bar for summer custodial workers and personally met with each parent or child who came up to the school. Aleno also scheduled meetings with district office staff. The curriculum director, the pupil personnel manager, and the treasurer all met with him. However, the superintendent ignored his requests.

He quickly learned his new boss's preference for spending the summer months at his lakeside cabin. Other principals told him that the superintendent didn't believe in "rocking the boat" in this well-regarded district. The trick, as they explained it, was to "work around" the superintendent by always filing glowing reports well in advance of the due date and attending to almost every district-assigned task in a perfunctory way. In other words, Aleno learned to manage his boss. By giving him what he needed to manage public relations, Aleno was able to rise above the ineffectiveness of district leadership and attend to his own priorities for innovation. In many ways Hood Elementary thrived under this system. As Aleno suggested, "Sometimes being cut off is a good thing. I fly under the radar. I just get what I need to do what I want."

Ample evidence from districts across the country suggests that when leadership is ineffective at the district and school level, teachers and students suffer (Leithwood, Louis, Anderson, & Wahlstrom, 2004). Ineffective leadership in schools and school districts is, however, probably more common than you think. In our research, we are often surprised to discover how little the district office personnel know about what happens in individual school buildings. We found that most schools had not been visited by a district office administrator more than once during the past year (and most of those visits were brief). Just as building leaders can fall prey to the pressures of daily tasks, so can district leaders—though in some cases this means that building leaders are left adrift. How many principals like it also often surprise us: by "flying under the radar," many principals feel free to create school cultures as they wish.

In our experience, effective building leaders manage ineffective district leadership by engaging in the following behaviors:

- *Connecting with other principals* to remain aware of important deadlines, state initiatives, grants, and new ideas. Absent an internal structure to support their needs, principals must create parallel arrangements (e.g., e-mails, phone messages, and after-school gatherings) to support their efforts. While this kind of network hardly qualifies as the administrator professional community that we argued for in the previous chapter, it fills a management hole.
- *Focusing on external support networks* rather than internal resources, including county office (regional or intermediate educational unit) professional development offerings and meetings, as well as capitalizing on the faculty resources available at local universities and colleges. (We say more about external networks and community relations in the next chapter.)
- *Going along* with the favorite projects of district leaders if they are not too distracting. If, unexplainably, the superintendent is a big fan of the school spelling bee, hold it. Public support for the superintendent's

wishes while not compromising internal goals is reasonable—and fortunately, at least some kids love spelling bees.

- *Doing what is right*, keeping your head down and your results good. This was Ridge High's Principal Marin's reasonable response to years of so-so leadership from the superintendent. Supported by their peers, effective building leaders learn that rather than pleasing the superintendent, they can identify what matters, obtain the needed resources, and seek approval elsewhere.

MOVING FORWARD

So how can you cultivate productive school-district relationships? Clearly, a first step involves observing and learning the culture of the district as a whole. If the culture is toxic, we don't suggest that you seek to single-handedly remedy the ills. The best choice may be to fly under the radar until things change. However, most districts do not have a toxic culture. Most districts, like most schools, have cultures where well-meaning, hard-working people would like things to be better. They often lack the skills to know how or the depth of relationships that can help to build broad support for change. So how does a school that "gets it" move ahead?

Focusing on intensifying leadership and building strong resilient cultures can go a long way to helping schools and districts achieve the results they seek. The suggestions below are not exhaustive but are derived from (1) the experiences of the principals whose cases we have presented in this book, (2) the emerging research on school-district relationships, and (3) the principles underlying our cultural framework:

- *Clarify expectations bilaterally.* You can begin to do this by creating a clear mutual understanding of what is expected. Stating your vision, listing the goals by which results will be measured, and providing unambiguous messages about the ways in which you plan to act all contribute to building trust.
- *Establish common values and priorities*, and negotiate arenas of acceptable difference. The principle of "we're all different but we're all expected to be good" requires a common core, but with almost everything else available for customization. Be clear about what you want to sign on for in the district's agenda. If the district's agenda is unclear, find the areas of agreement.
- *Design opportunities for communication and mutual learning.* If school leaders are to meet goals, members of the administrative team must learn together. Dialogue concerning "the good, the bad and the ugly" should be honest, open, and regular whenever possible. If district communication continues to be weak, "fly beneath the radar" but build connections with other principals (or allies in the district office).
- *Build trust.* Open communication is an important underpinning of trust, but you also need to make sure that you are seen as a reliable

team member whenever it is possible. If spelling bees or upbeat reports are the only way you can achieve that, the basis for trust will be limited. See if you can find other ways to work in concert with the district, as long as it does not distort what your teachers and students need most.

- *Coach and model a culture of professionalism.* You can actively work to model the behaviors you expect of others, and provide by example a bridge between the expectations of the district and school. You can also develop stories that describe how the work of the district and the school will build on each other and reinforce the school's goals (see Chapter 4), and tell them to the district staff and your teachers.

- *Plan and think strategically.* Because setting clear directions and measures of progress are fundamental to school improvement, school leaders need to employ strategic planning and thinking in tactical and deliberate ways. Strategic assessments of your school's context (uniqueness) and progress (toward common goals) should be part of the regular and ongoing dialogue between you and the district, and should help keep everyone "on track" in balancing any tensions that exist.

CONCLUSION

We wish to reiterate the importance of the school-district relationship in overall school effectiveness. In the best places, district and building leadership are aligned toward goals that complement one another and maintain a focus on school improvement. We have found that when building and district leaders attend to achieving a critical mass of the strategies listed below, relationships can flourish and school and district cultures become more productive. Even in districts where things are not perfect but they fall short of toxicity, the following main points still hold.

1. School leaders are unavoidably part of and influenced by the districts in which they work.

2. Developing close alliances is part of intensifying leadership. When these center on teaching and learning, opportunities to help students are dramatically increased.

3. When temporary toxicity occurs, successful principals keep the home fires burning and seek ways to work within the system by flying under the radar until things improve while connecting with other like-minded positive leaders.

4. School-district relationships benefit from attention to PCOLT attributes in the same ways schools benefit from attention to them. As professionalism, community, shared learning, and trust grow across the district, leadership intensifies and strong positive cultures emerge.

REFLECTIONS

1. Reread the boxed chapter objectives. What can you do almost immediately to improve your relationship with the district?

    List the knowledge and skills that you already have that will support you in moving forward.

    List three to five action steps you can take to begin your work.

    List three to five people or groups of people you can engage in this effort.

    List the ways these ideas and people support the core vision and goals of your school.

2. Do a quick diagnosis of the district's culture. Answer the following questions:

    What is the level of trust and/or conflict among staff?

    Are districtwide instructional and curricular decisions openly discussed?

    Do central office staff value each other and do they work together well?

    Are districtwide communication structures open and honest?

    Is learning something in which everyone is engaged or is it what the kids do?

    Who makes most of the decisions in the district? What happens if people don't agree with a decision that has been made?

    Do people seem to like working here? Who, if anyone, seems to be dissatisfied?

3. Once you have answered the questions above, list the issues you have discovered about your district culture.

    Where are the allies for your school culture efforts?

    Where are the barriers?

    Where are district resources that would be helpful in supporting your efforts?

    Who has knowledge that can support your work?

    Who has contacts that can support your work?

4. What are the disadvantages to flying beneath the radar? How can principals that temporarily need to take cover find support? How can principals who have chosen to avoid temporary toxicity become part of the larger district culture when times get better?

ANALYZING YOUR SCHOOL

Diagnosing Your District Culture

Consider the following items. Assess the relationship between the district office and building leadership efforts. Where are your sources of internal support? Where might reaching out to external mentors and coaches be needed?

In my district . . .	Always	Sometimes	Never
A high level of trust exists between central office staff and building leadership teams.			
Communication is regular, clear, and focused on school and student success.			
Central office staff view learning about new initiatives and ideas as part of their role.			
Decision making is open and transparent.			
When problems arise in the district, the central office can be counted on to help.			
Central office staff offers opportunities for professional learning and development.			
Instructional and curricular matters are a prominent topic of discussion.			
People like coming to the district office for events; they are always worthwhile.			
Central office staff supports school improvement agendas and efforts.			
Resources are provided to support school culture change efforts.			

Schools and Communities

Working With the Enduring
Dilemmas of Time and Accountability

Chapters 5 and 6 emphasized the value of building alliances and expanding your professional networks. Professional colleagues are not, however, the only important members of your widening network of partners. This chapter focuses on how to work with other important groups and individuals that affect your school.

In this chapter you will learn about:

- working with members of your local school council or other parent and community groups with an established role in influencing your school;
- coordinating with human service agencies that serve your student and family population;
- working with parents to engage them more fully in the education of their children;
- working with members of the broader community to access resources that can support student learning and development; and
- engaging with community leaders and the media so that your school's operations are transparent and well understood.

UNCOMFORTABLE—BUT IMPORTANT

You probably didn't decide to become a school leader because you were drawn to any of the above job requirements. Surveys of principals over the years have consistently pointed out that their greatest job satisfaction comes from the work that they do inside the school. This is, apparently, not simply a function of the current emphasis on instructional leadership. William Gray, writing nearly a century ago, decried tasks that draw principals away from focusing on supporting teachers and good classroom instruction as "administrative distractions" (Gray, 1918). More recently, a survey of all principals in one state found that the greatest job satisfaction came from the rapport that they developed with students and teachers, while the major problem area in communication came from working with families (DiPaola & Tschannen-Moran, 2003).

Around the world, policy pressures from the state and federal governments have changed the role of school leaders. Rather than being accountable for school results to the local community, principals are increasingly hired (and even fired) based on their success in helping teachers to raise scores on state-developed achievement tests. The sense of conflicted accountability—local school council, the priorities of elected local boards, or state annual yearly progress ratings—is pervasive according to one comprehensive study of secondary school principals (Goodwin, Cunningham, & Childress, 2003), and make the job more difficult. Because this shift is relatively recent, the school leadership literature has paid less attention to school-community relationships than to school-district relationships.

At the beginning of the nineteenth century, most schools were located in small towns where there were only one or two schools, and where the school professionals were participants in the community. The underlying assumption—that the management of school-community relationships can be based on informal meetings over coffee and membership in the local Rotary Club seems quaint for many of today's younger practitioners. But textbooks for principal preparation courses rarely reveal practical advice about how to work with parents and the community, and specialized books devoted to the subject often have a distinct public relations focus. We hope to convince you that neither perfunctory memberships in local organizations nor public relations are appropriate models for school-community relations in today's world.

As state and federal accountability systems have gathered steam, community ties are often one of the weakest and least prioritized components of principal practice (Goldring & Hausman, 2001). It is no wonder that principals feel conflicted over time spent in community engagement. A 2003 survey of teachers, parents, and principals found that principals rate the importance of working with the community far lower than with teachers and students (MetLife, 2003), while another survey of a different group reported that parent involvement was ranked as 21st of 31 priority areas of work—only above tasks such as becoming more up to date on computers and expanding the curriculum beyond state requirements (Whitaker & Turner, 2000). Research on the effects of Chicago's decentralization of responsibility for selecting principals to local school councils resulted in principal reports that they were spending more time that ever on community relations, but believed that they should be spending less (Bryk, Sebring, Kerbow, Rollow, & Easton, 1998).

Report after report urges principals to spend more time on instructional leadership rather than developing external relationships. However, communities (not just parents) are an important resource for improving schools. This chapter will illustrate community and parent-involvement programs that meet multiple purposes—all of which can be consistent with the other roles that principals are expected to play.

COMMUNITY AND PARENT INVOLVEMENT: WHY DO YOU WANT IT? WHAT CAN YOU DO?*

If you look through various electronic search engines using keywords such as *community*, *school*, and *involvement*, the topic is clearly popular. We have organized the research in this area into five major themes: (1) improved student learning and development; (2) schools as agencies of democracy; (3) building social capital to support student and community development; (4) schools as responsible actors with a moral obligation to contribute to communities, especially underserved groups; and (5) linking schools and communities to boost school self-interest. In our work, each of these themes can be associated with statements that appear either in written articles or in conversations with professionals and community members. To illustrate the meaning of the themes, Table 7.1 presents typical statements for each of them.

We now turn to exploring each of these themes, by including illustrative programs and practices, and examining their utility in helping us further understand intensified leadership and cultural change efforts.

Student Learning and Development: A Foundation

Most (though not all) writers presume that student learning and development are the ultimate reason to improve school-community relationships. There are, however, differences in the way in which this desired outcome is defined. A large number of writers look at cognitive achievement, but usually emphasize parent involvement over broader community involvement (Desimone, Finn-Stevenson, & Henrich, 2000; Morris, 2002; Sheldon, 2003). The link between parent involvement and student achievement is well established (Burke, 2001) but remains an underutilized

---

*This section is based on earlier work that Karen Seashore Louis carried out with Kathryn Riley in 2004 (Riley & Louis, 2004).

Table 7.1   Assumptions Underlying the Organizing Framework

Focus/Theme	Schools and communities need to be more closely linked so that . . .
Student achievement: Improving student learning and academic development	1. Children learn to become more responsible. 2. Teachers understand more about where children come from and what motivates children. 3. The curriculum will be more relevant for pupils. 4. Teachers and parents can work together more closely and help pupils to achieve.
Schools as agencies for democracy: Making schools more accountable and increasing democratic involvement	5. Schools will be more accountable to their local community. 6. Local people can have more of a say in important decisions about their schools. 7. They can come together to plan for what they want for children. 8. Young people have more opportunities to be involved in decisions about their lives. 9. Children have a sense of belonging in their community.
Building social capital: Building social capital within communities, by encouraging schools to collaborate to promote community well being (e.g., healthier and safer communities)	10. Vandalism and antisocial behavior among young people is reduced. 11. The local area is safer, healthier, and more attractive. 12. Adults as well as children are encouraged to learn. 13. Parents feel included in their child's education.
Schools as moral agents in the community: Schools as actors in the broader effort to create a more just and equitable society	14. They can work together to tackle racism and other forms of discrimination. 15. Business and human service leaders will work with schools to improve the chances for young people. 16. Schools can do more to prepare new immigrant groups to take part in society. 17. They can agree on fundamental values relating to education.
School self-interest: Promoting schools' self-interest through the development of good public relations	18. Discipline and behavior within schools is improved. 19. Schools employ more people who understood the local community. 20. People have more information that could help them support a school.

SOURCE: Adapted from K. Riley & K. S. Louis (2004). *Exploring new forms of community leadership: Linking schools and communities to improve educational opportunities for young people.* Unpublished report to the National College for School Leadership.

approach to school improvement in most schools, particularly in secondary schools and urban areas (Gonzalez-DeHass & Willems, 2003). Much of the attention focuses on the obstacles that inhibit increased parent engagement and emphasize the perceived decline in parent support and involvement.

But do you really think that parents care less about their children today than they did previously? Ample evidence suggests that this is not the case—and that most poor and immigrant parents (those who are hardest to involve) value education as deeply as did previous immigrant groups. As educators, what we have not always done is to consider seriously how schools (and school leaders) can change the ways in which schools connect to families to take into consideration two-career/multijob families, as well as a changing demographic composition that confronts almost every school district these days.

One of the pioneers in this area is Joyce Epstein. Since the 1980s, her work has emphasized the importance of investigating and building on overlapping spheres of influence of families and schools on students' learning and development and on family and school effectiveness (Epstein & Dauber, 1991). One of her major contributions has been to move beyond parent conferences and back-to-school nights, emphasizing six different ways in which parents and schools can complement each other (Table 7.2).

Table 7.2   Epstein's Framework for Parent-School Collaboration

Types	Definitions
Type 1: Parenting	Helping all families establish supportive home environments for children
Type 2: Communicating	Establishing two-way exchanges about school programs and children's progress
Type 3: Volunteering	Recruiting and organizing parent help at school, home, or other locations
Type 4: Learning at home	Providing information and ideas to families about how to help students with homework and other curriculum-related materials
Type 5: Decision making	Having parents from all backgrounds serve as representatives and leaders in school committees
Type 6: Collaborating with the community	Identifying and integrating resources and services from the community to strengthen school programs

SOURCE: Adapted from J. L. Epstein, M. G. Sanders, B. S. Simon, K. C. Salinas, N. R. Jansorn, & F. L. Van Voorhis. (2002). *School, family, and community partnerships: Your handbook for action* (2nd ed.). Thousand Oaks, CA: Corwin Press.

Epstein's work provides a singular array of resources for thoughtful administrators who wish to adapt her ideas to their settings, and her Web site is noted in the resource section for this chapter. Significantly, if you look at the types listed above, you can see that most require active work on the part of a school leader if they are to occur. Take for example Epstein's Type 1: Support for parenting. Though principals certainly would not be expected to lead parenting sessions, we have never been in a school where they were in place without active efforts on the part of the principal to secure the resources to make these activities happen. Type 2, communicating, is primarily the job of the teacher. Teacher preparation programs are, however, generally weak in giving teachers the skills to work effectively with parents. Typically it is principals who help ensure access to job-embedded professional development that is directly linked to the kinds of families and parents that the school serves. These are only two examples that suggest how central the principal is to getting this work "front and center" in the school's daily practice.

Engaging parents has always been easier in elementary schools than in upper grade levels, and Epstein's work has focused primarily on engaging families with younger children. The work of Sandra Christenson and her colleagues expands the array of tested programs to include upper grade students as well. While Christenson's "Check & Connect" program is featured on the federal government's "What Works" Web site as a dropout prevention program (see resource section for more information), she advocates a broader engagement strategy in which families, community service providers, and schools collaborate to support individual students who have fragile connections to school. Creating connections that avoid even a temporary loss of engagement allows students to become successful both in middle and high school. The programs that they have designed have resulted in:

- decreased truancy,
- decreased dropout rates,
- increased accrual of credits,
- increased school completion, and
- an impact on literacy.

The main emphasis of the program is on consistent identification of students who may be temporarily in need of support (checking), and the development of communication systems, steered from a base in the school, that keep all relevant adults in the loop (connecting) (Table 7.3). Particularly important for many of today's schools are the significant effects of the program on students with various disabilities—a population that has become increasingly important in today's accountability environment (Sinclair, Christenson, & Thurlow, 2005).

Table 7.3   Christenson's Framework for Home-School Collaboration

Elements	Definitions
Element 1: Relationship Building	Mutual trust and open communication, nurtured through a long-term commitment focused on students' educational success.
Element 2: Routine Monitoring of Alterable Indicators	Systemically checking warning signs of withdrawal (attendance, academic performance, behavior) that are readily available to school personnel and that can be altered through intervention.
Element 3: Individualized and Timely Intervention	Support tailored to individual student needs, based on level of engagement with school, associated influences of home and school, and the leveraging of local resources.
Element 4: Long-Term Commitment	Committing to students and families for at least two years, including the ability to follow highly mobile youth from school to school and program to program.
Element 5: Persistence Plus	A persistent source of academic motivation, a continuity of familiarity with the youth and family, and a consistency in the message that "education is important for your future."
Element 6: Problem Solving	Designed to promote the acquisition of skills to resolve conflict constructively and to look for solutions rather than a source of blame.
Element 7: Affiliation With School and Learning	Facilitating students' access to and active participation in school-related activities and events.

SOURCE: Adapted from Check & Connect (http://ies.ed.gov/ncee/wwc/index.asp).

How does Check & Connect change the school? The answer is that it is successful in large part because it does not disrupt the usual day-to-day classroom work of teachers and students, nor does it ask teachers to take a great deal of time away from their students to work directly with parents. What changes is the allocation of resources, because a trained mentor or advocate, whose responsibility is to ensure that the connections between the various agencies and individuals who can support the fragile student occur, does most of the "heavy lifting." Teachers—particularly secondary school teachers who see upward of sixty students a week and who cannot possibly engage in the home visits that are recommended by some school reformers—are grateful that someone is caring for the students most at-risk in their classrooms. Administrators who monitor discipline are relieved of many tasks, and parents develop trusting relationships with a stable person in the school. Thus, what changes is the culture of the school; everyone feels more confident that the students who are in need will be helped, and the nagging sense of inadequacy that lies within many teachers' hearts is alleviated. Of course, this cannot happen unless administrators are willing to take on the very difficult task of rearranging the school's staff to include the salary of a mentor/advocate. This may mean cuts in other areas or negotiating with the district to use salary lines for something other than what they are currently used for. Only administrators who see parent engagement as a priority will be willing to risk this effort.

Parent and community involvement is increasingly embedded as a component of whole-school school improvement efforts that are specifically focused on improving achievement (Clark & Clark, 2002; Sheldon, 2003). The emphasis in many of these initiatives is on direct involvement (for example, having parents monitor homework for completion and accuracy), but there is also attention to the ways in which parents can indirectly improve learning; for example, by increasing attendance or other behaviors that are known to be associated with higher achievement (Epstein & Sheldon, 2002; Sheldon & Epstein, 2005). The whole-school reform model developed by Yale psychologist James Comer is probably the best-known, but the principles embodied in his work are visible in most of the other whole-school models that embrace community as part of change.

PRINCIPLES UNDERLYING COMER'S WHOLE-SCHOOL REFORM

The Comer process is an educational change initiative based on the principles of child, adolescent, and adult development. It mobilizes teachers, administrators, parents, and other concerned adults to support students' personal, social, and academic growth. It also helps them make better programmatic and curriculum decisions based on students' needs and developmental principles. The Comer process in not a project add-on, but rather an operating system—a way of managing, organizing, coordinating, and integrating activities. SDP practices considered highly controversial in 1969—whole-school change, school-based management, strong parent involvement in decision making, and teacher study groups—are now common in schools throughout the country (Joyner, Comer, & Ben-Avie, 2004).

The fundamentals of the Comer process include strong management and planning leadership at the school sites, but also a central student support team that links to other human services in the community, as well as input from (and to) parents. In other words, at the core of the Comer model is a form of intensified leadership that includes teachers, schools' social workers or counselors, and other people who have little experience working in schools. Engaging people in new alliances is challenging; there are differences in language and professional codes that need to be negotiated and different assumptions about priorities. If the principal is not actively involved in this work, these intensified school-community teams tend to founder, even when everyone agrees that they are essential for student academic success.

While the Comer model is one of the best-established whole-school reforms, these basic principles have been incorporated into many other research-based models that are more appropriate for older students. Unfortunately, whole-school reform models that emphasize parent and community involvement seem weaker in their instructional focus than other school reform models (Borman, Hewes, Overman, & Brown, 2003). There are also many smaller-scale local initiatives to increase parent and community involvement, ranging from including using computers to network schools and parents, business partnerships between schools and local employers that are intended to ease transition to employment, and service learning initiatives that bring students into the community to change and learn from their environment (Chen & Dym, 2003; Sanders, 2003). In spite of Sanders's efforts to categorize the parent-involvement literature, one is left with the clear impression that (aside from the well-funded whole-school reform activities) there is a great deal of activity based on good intentions rather than broader principles or theories that might become the basis for school-community involvement.

This suggests that aside from the work of Epstein and Christenson and their colleagues, a great deal of the homegrown wisdom embodied in individual programs and some of the comprehensive school reforms still focuses on ways of involving parents and families that are based on aspiration rather than research. Thus, hoping that an "off the shelf" package can program your leadership decisions is misplaced. You will need to understand the fundamental principles school-community engagement to guide it and make it make it work in your school.

In many schools, staff members are discouraged and see the task as too difficult. Efforts to increase parent involvement are not always successful, particularly when the schools in question are in challenging communities with diverse populations (Brain & Reid, 2003; Collignon, Men, & Sereri, 2001; Moosa, Karabenick, & Adams, 2001; Nakagawa, Stafford, Fisher, & Matthews, 2002). Race, ethnicity, and social class form a common subtext in these discussions, which emphasize the differences between the culture of teachers and the culture of the parent and student communities. The absence in many of the articles of solid theories of action that incorporate consideration of both the characteristics of the strategy and the specific community context may account for the limited results.

In our experience, schools in challenging circumstances can have success in involving parents and the community, but unless the internal school culture and leadership are strong, these may be isolated. Let us contrast two schools—one elementary, and one high school—in the same district.

THE NINTH-GRADE TEAM AT LAKESIDE HIGH

The team was established by the principal (a Native American) to address the high truancy and dropout rates among the lower-income minority students (mainly Native Americans) at Lakeside. With his support, the ninth-grade team worked hard to create a coherent integrated curriculum that was strong on fusing the arts with social studies and English. They focused on a mask-making project that encouraged students to explore their emotions when making a mask of themselves, and then led the students into related writing activities. The special education teacher (whom the principal had assigned to be a core member of the team) led a writing activity using an except from the Jim Carrey movie *The Mask*; the English teacher used a different stimulus, but with a similar goal. Later, the teachers and principal agreed to use the school library to create an exhibit of the masks and student writing. Parents were asked to come and see the exhibit, and, while they were there, to attend parent-teacher conferences. Because the students were extremely proud of their work, they were enthusiastic proponents of parent attendance, which was consequently much higher than it had previously been.

The principal was not a highly visible player in this small effort to change the lives of a few students and their families because that was not his style. He was an essential feature nonetheless. First, he promoted the ninth-grade team idea, and built a core of PCOLT by ensuring this team's continuity of membership over several years. Second, he allocated resources—much of the school's arts-partner funding—to work with the ninth graders, rather than rewarding the AP English class with a Shakespeare trip. Third, he supported the exhibition of student work in a very public fashion in the symbolic center of learning—the library. He also lent his cultural understanding to the design of the team's effort to engage parents, largely high-school dropouts, who were notoriously reluctant to come to "back-to-school nights." He didn't command, but his support was always in the background—which paid off in the almost 80 percent reenrollment of the most at-risk students as tenth graders. Successes like these reverberated far beyond the five teachers who were involved on the team.

Lakeview Elementary provides a sobering contrast.

LAKEVIEW ELEMENTARY AND PARENT INVOLVEMENT

Lakeview (which we first introduced in Chapter 4) had a long tradition of connections with the predominantly African American community in which it was situated. In fact, the teachers and the former principal, Artie Simmons, simply assumed that this was a deeply engrained part of "who we are." After Simmons, who was well known among all parents (and former parents) left the school, it became apparent that he was the attractor. Some of the most active parents began to enroll their children in charter schools, including one that emphasized its ability to provide culturally sensitive learning environments with an Afrocentric component. The parents who remained seemed to be less stable and less likely to come to school events.

The new principal, Katie Harms, instructed all of the grade-level teams to plan for special event evenings that would bring parents and students back to talk about the curriculum. These were not, for the most part, successful. One teacher commented: "I mean, we had ours last week and I think we had really fun evening planned! And I had two (parents come) and (my teaching partner) had two and (our other teammate) had one. So we did all this work but . . . you know, it was great for those five families." However, in the same building, other teachers described a very different experience: "I told (my students) we were having GIANT cupcakes. Not little cupcakes, giant cupcakes, and we were having juice! What I do is make sure it is a big deal and I hand out a lot of notices. The more notices I send out, the bigger deal I make of it, the greater turnout I get. So I get what I get out of it because of what I put into it." However, there was so little communication between teams in this small school that teachers never discussed ideas about how to make the events work better in all teams.

SOURCE: Adapted from C. N. Zwicky. (2008). *Pushed or pulled? Between school mobility among experienced teachers.* Unpublished doctoral thesis, University of Minnesota, Minneapolis.

The problem at Lakeview was twofold. First, the principal assumed that the teachers were expert at involving parents because of the school's history, but in the past, the principal had been the main attractor. In other words, the new principal didn't bother to learn the underlying cultural assumptions of the school and didn't take her responsibility for direct engagement seriously. Second, the teachers lacked PCOLT and, because they didn't talk much within the school, they rarely learned from each other. Good ideas and practices, which might have begun to substitute for the absence of the avuncular former principal, remained isolated within teams.

Up to now, we have looked primarily at efforts to increase parent and community involvement that are directly tied to student achievement. Other authors take a somewhat different view; embedding student development in a broader definition of learning outcomes, such as pupil leadership, cultural competence, or citizenship development (Edgar, Patton,

& Day-Vines, 2002; Wallin, 2003), supporting healthy students (Marx & Northrop, 2000), or simply enlarging students' informal learning. A theme in some of the research is using parents and community not simply as a supplement to in-school academic work, but to actually reform the school itself by changing the curriculum (Clark & Clark, 2002).

Reforms that go beyond simple parent involvement activities represent a shift in the cultural assumptions about whom the school "belongs to." The core supposition in most schools is that educational professionals have expertise and skills, and that in most cases students and families should be socialized to align with their judgment about how schools and classrooms should be organized. While most of the programs for community and parent engagement don't presume that teachers need to make *radical* changes in what they do, they suggest that thinking about how students learn should be *broadened* to incorporate learning opportunities beyond a particular classroom and a particular school, It does not make teachers and principals responsible for student's and family's lives, but the underlying assumption is that teachers will be more successful in their own practice to the extent that they blend professional expertise with community-based knowledge and practice. In the process, good things can happen for kids and school culture.

Whether or not you can incorporate these or similar reforms in your school, there are important lessons to be learned from the mix of research findings about parent and community involvement:

- Involved and knowledgeable parents play a significant role in supporting whole-child development.
- Programs that focus on increasing family support for student's development, like those developed by Epstein and Christenson, may have payoff for long-term student success, particularly for struggling students.
- Parent and community involvement in schools as a short-term strategy for improving student test scores may sidetrack efforts to increase student achievement, and may be seen by parents as manipulative or misaligned with their goals for their child.
- School leaders who wish intensify leadership by including parents and community members in more active roles in the school should consider options that do not place excessive additional demands on teachers, as they are likely to be involved in other school or district efforts that focus on their instructional practices.

Schools as Agencies for Democracy

Parents and communities support schools by encouraging student learning and development, but the relationship can be more than merely functional. One major vehicle involves school accountability to local constituencies, and thus intersects with efforts to decentralize and create site-based management councils. In its narrowest sense, democratic community involvement is seen as a way of ensuring that local values are reflected in resource allocation decisions or in developing indicators of improvement that go beyond those established by states (Chavkin, 2000; Sokoloff, 2001). Indirect community involvement is also supported by policies that allow parents to create intentional communities by choosing among schools. The assumption is that when people are allowed to choose, they become more involved in the life of the school (volunteerism) than if they are merely assigned to a school (Houle, 2002).

This relatively passive view of the democratic purposes of schools is challenged by those who argue for the importance of broader public participation in a wide variety of issues facing educators (Louis, 2003; Wilson, Iverson, & Chrastil, 2001). The democratic view of community involvement emphasizes both accountability and responsibility to the public and a more active role in creating democratic structures. In England, the development of Education Action Zones in low-income communities emphasized the need to include the voices of marginalized groups by distributing rights and responsibilities to groups outside the school (McGuire, 2000).

Real democratic involvement of this type is not easy to achieve (Sanders, 2001). Community members may be too busy, and a truncated form of consultation and involvement rather than full participation may result (Vollmer, 2001). Minority groups must be empowered if full partnership and active engagement is to emerge, and efforts to do so may be hampered by the absence of indigenous staff members (Delany & Wenmoth, 2001).

Community members must feel a real sense of ownership of the schools, which is difficult to maintain in larger communities, if they are to remain strongly supportive and involved. The more diffuse and diverse the community, the harder it is to obtain productive democratic involvement (Louis, 2003; Wieland, 2001). Maintaining involvement requires strong relationship-building activities that go beyond the usual (Mapp, 2003), and all efforts may be disrupted by power and ideology, which inevitably arise in participatory settings and which when activated cannot always be confined to a single issue or choice.

A strong leadership theme emerges in these descriptions, in part because it is school leaders who are accountable for the attainment of educational goals, and in part because of their traditional responsibility for managing the interface between schools and the public (Sanders & Harvey, 2002; Wilson, et al., 2001). Among the most poignant images of how leaders do this work are some of the video clips that are easily available from the George Lucas Foundation (listed in the resources), where a quick search for community partnerships brings up several that are among our favorites.

SCHOOLS THAT ENGAGE WHOLE COMMUNITIES

Though the principal at Capitol Elementary had described the community as "dying," her door-to-door work in getting support for the school's development has created a vibrant campus with active participation in both formal and informal decision making. Given the district's initial plans to close the school, as well as a community profile that was predominantly low-income and transient, her door-to-door work to get parents and small-business partners involved to save the school suggests the power of the individual to create broadly intensified leadership for improvement.

At the secondary level, the West Hawaii Explorations Academy (a small school or choice) and Bio-Tech Academy, a small learning community in Andrew Squires High School in San Jose, both focus on problem-based learning where mentoring and supervision of student activities is provided by community members, and where teachers work to connect student learning projects with community service and real-life problems. The Minnesota Business Academy, a charter school, was designed by employers and teachers to ensure that both university-bound and more vocationally oriented students would have opportunities to work in real internship settings outside of the school. (Videos of these and other community-engaged schools can be found at http://www.edutopia.org/video?q=video&filter0=69&filter1.)

What is the common denominator in these schools? The main difference between them and more "usual" schools is that they have exceptionally permeable boundaries: principals, students, teachers, and community members work seamlessly to help the schools to incorporate educational experiences that are valued by their communities. For both elementary and secondary schools, the point is not that community members and parents are represented on site councils, but that they participate meaningfully in the education of students. The democratic school, in these instances, is one in which the professional expertise of teachers and school administrators is respected, but where they do not have all the answers to the puzzle of how children learn.

In sum, the level of trust between school staff and involved community members is exceptional, but is not focused only on parent involvement. The culture of the school has changed (or, in the case of new schools, was part of the original design) to make real leadership opportunities available to many members of community. In the cases described above, broad community engagement was at least initially dependent on the active and persistent efforts of the principal to reach out and cement interest in participation. In the case of new schools (like the Minnesota Business Academy), the community was part of the initial design team, while in the case of revitalizing schools, like the one described below, the principal tirelessly solicited involvement in planning from community partners.

COMMUNITIES AND SCHOOL DESIGN

The Las Vegas school district is one of the fastest growing in the United States and has expanded over the past three decades from a largely white and middle-class district of about 50,000 students to a projected enrollment of nearly half a million by 2014, an increasingly number of which are poor and minority. C. P. Squires Elementary has an ESL population of nearly 97 percent but has organized itself around the principles of community schooling. Parents are told that they must be active in teaching their children Spanish, while the school will take care of teaching English. Parents can attend English classes in the middle school across the street, while their younger preschool children learn letters and are introduced to English in after-school programs taught by certified teachers. Community volunteers from both businesses and the burgeoning retirement community serve as mentors to school-age children, and a wide variety of after-school programs keep many children in school beyond the regular day. The school houses a health clinic that it shares with three other nearby schools. Title I provides funding for full-day kindergarten, but the school is not a hothouse. Instead it reflects the strong efforts by both district and school leaders to harness the energy of the community to create a supportive environment for children and families (see http://www.edu topia.org/las-vegas-c-p-squires-elementary for more detailed information).

The principals in all the schools that we have looked at play a crucial role in whether efforts to engage the community go well or badly, in particular because, unless there is a great deal of trust, the bumps in the road will result in conflict and politics rather than problem solving. Megan Tschannen-Moran puts it succinctly: "The behavior of principals plays a critical role in setting the tone of trust within a school. If you hope to benefit from the rewards of a trusting culture, it is your responsibility to initiate trusting relationships" (Tschannen-Moran, 2004, p. 37). Peggy Bryan, the principal of Sherman Oaks Elementary School, claims that her willingness to admit that she was *not* an expert was a decided advantage:

Well, what I brought to the table when we were trying to figure out what to do is—I brought a lot of ignorance. I just owned the fact that I didn't know how to do it. The schools I had worked with prior to [Sherman Oaks] didn't make any headway really on gaining parent participation or community involvement. So, I just said, "You know, I don't know how to do it." That was our starting point. So our collective claim on not knowing what to do led us to an organization, a community activist organization called PACT, which is Parents Acting in Community Together. And we said to them, "We don't know how to do this. Can you teach us?" And they did. (Edutopia, n.d.-b)

Intensified leadership requires principals to abandon any notion that they are "the deciders." The fluid nature of democratic participation and its somewhat unpredictable consequences complicate the lives of school leaders (Leonardo, 2003). Traditionally, the school leader is expected to protect the "core technology" of the school from interference by outsiders, including community members (Rosenblum, Louis, & Rossmiller, 1994), and the increasing need to distribute real responsibility outside school walls is not always favorably regarded by school staff members. Thus, making schools more open and more democratic represents a much greater challenge to the culture of the school than the simpler parent-involvement strategies that are most visible in most schoolwide reform models. Nevertheless, when the principal is truly committed, intensified leadership is the consequence. Principal Peggy Bryan summed up her experiences creating a successful community school by commenting that what she was most proud of was the "leadership that's been built. Again starting by actually handing over the leadership to the parents right off the bat. That's come back through on all angles. The staff, they can go any-where and promote this school" (Edutopia, n.d.-b).

The lessons for school leaders are both obvious and subtle, and include:

- Building a more democratic school involves making schools more permeable and open.
- Inviting more people into the school, and sending students out of the school for learning experiences, requires establishing stronger trusting relationships, both within and outside the school.
- Trusting relationships among teachers and between teachers and parents/community has a major impact on school culture that is positive for students.
- More real democracy means more risk—but a potentially higher payoff in support for schools.

Social Capital and Civic Capacity: Healthy Communities, Healthy Schools

Schools cannot provide children with all of the support they need to learn. The concept of social capital refers directly to the well-established finding that people who have stronger and more resilient networks of rela-tionships with other people are healthier, happier, and live longer. For children, this means that they have multiple supportive relationships with adults and institutions that support their development, and that the adults in their lives know and work with each other. Social capital is one of the factors that is most frequently identified with children's and adolescent resilience—their capacity to cope with both small and large disturbances in their lives (Cairns & Cairns, 1994). The greater the child's social capital, the less likely it is that there will be breaks in the safety net through which they may fall. A related concept—civic capacity—points to the obvious fact that some settings have more resources to provide social capital than others. Schools can either accept the community as it is, with whatever inadequacies it contains, or they can take their place in a perspective that emphasizes community development. As Ellen Goldring and Charles Hausman point out, "community development initiatives embrace a perspective that suggests that schools and their communities must be linked in multiple avenues, multiple spaces, and multiple activities" (Goldring & Hausman, 2001, p. 194).

While the democratic ideal discussed above focuses on decision making and participation around the core tasks of education, a social capital perspective emphasizes a broader contribution of community social networks and relationships to the functioning of the school. Hill (2001), for example, argues that it is important to "break the hermetic seal" around the school in order to gain access to the human and cultural resources that exist in all but the most dysfunctional communities (see also Morris, 2002).

Social capital, resilience, and civic capacity all focus on the assumption that every community has *assets* that can be accessed for the purpose of supporting children and youth. The concepts—and the attendant actions that schools must take to find and develop assets—stand in stark contrast to a more typical *deficit* model that looks at nontraditional family structures, economic decline and joblessness, or the presence of many immigrant groups with different agendas and values as creating cumulative odds for community support. This, of course, represents a major cultural shift for many educators, who see communities as a context over which they have little or no influence.

One important feature of this cultural change is that most schools that are deeply vested in building social capital have also entered into partnerships with other agencies in which they have essentially two leaders: one from an agency in the community and the school's principal.

PS 218—A MIDDLE SCHOOL SHARING LEADERSHIP

Luis Malave, the principal of a middle school in New York that partnered with the Children's Aid Society to provide family and health services, adult, education and community programs, and before- and after-school enrichment experiences for students, is open about the rewards and challenges:

We share resources. We strategize together. We're on the school leadership team together. Basically we're inseparable right now. We're married in the figurative sense, for the duration of my tenure here. The reason why at times this can't go on in other

(Continued)

(Continued)

places is because there is a lack of trust, because there are territorial issues, there are even formalities in the way each entity operates. Social service agencies at times have a little bit less formality. The bureaucracy dictates to us [at the school] that we must be absolutely formal in every sense of the way. But those are things that are workable and we mitigate anything that needs to be mitigated and we just move on. (Edutopia, n.d.-a)

Malave is particularly enthusiastic about what might be called the paradox of community partnerships. By ceding autonomy, he gains flexibility:

Sometimes we have a person that we really want [to hire]. I can pay four hours. They [the Children's Aid Society] pay four hours. The person works full time, and that's a huge, huge benefit to us. The huge piece that I see here is that they bring a certain level of expertise in a variety of areas that we truly are desperate for, especially in mental health. We have a number of things that happened this year, especially with 9/11 and the plane crash, and we even had the death of a kid; it was truly a blessing to have Children's Aid Society and their social workers and the team of psychologists to help me cope with the numerous kids that were involved in those particular situations. (Edutopia, n.d.-a)

This case, like others involved in community schools, illustrates an important point about intensified leadership that we have made over and over: it is not the same as "delegating" or even "distributing," and it is more than "mutual influence." Intensification requires that people enter into real partnerships in which the responsibility for planning, decision making, and keeping the emerging culture alive genuinely belongs to multiple partners.

But as Luis Malave points out, this form of intensification complicates his life, and he even worries that about whether it will outlast his tenure as a principal. Why would you choose to do this, given that it may make your job more complex and has long-run rather than short-term payoffs for student achievement? There are multiple reasons.

Interest in social capital is increasing in part because of the global shifts in population that are bringing rapid increases in immigrants to areas that were previously homogeneous. Under these circumstances, looking for the positive features of the newcomers' cultures strikes many educators as preferable to a deficit model that emphasizes what newcomers lack (Brunn & Delaney-Barmann, 2001). The importance of social capital—whether or not it is identified by the label—is supported by studies that examine successful schools with large minority or poor populations. These studies find that social cohesiveness outside the school supports shared learning objectives, as well as helping to stabilize the political environment that creates significant challenges for urban schools (Hill, 2001).

Communities—including poor communities—are full of untapped resources that go beyond cohesive social relationships that provide caring support for children (Bauch, 2001). Shared norms and values that encourage learning may be unrecognized, and social institutions (such as faith organizations) may have programs that can be linked to school success. While finding cohesiveness in rural or homogeneous communities may be easier, in settings that are characterized by sociocultural tensions, a mix of democratic involvement and networking may provide significant contributions for school improvement (Leistyna, 2002). Furthermore, the assumption that all multiethnic cities have low social capital because of divisions and tensions is unwarranted. Cities with similar demographics vary significantly in their civic capacity to support schools (Stone, 2001).

Among strategies that promote social capital, the development of school-linked social services, such as that exemplified by PS 218, described above, is the best known (Goldring & Hausman, 2001). Whether services are colocated (within the school) or proximate and easily accessible, the idea that healthy families promote healthy schools (and vice versa) involves rethinking the segmented approach to public support for poor and minority-dominant communities (Marx & Northrop, 2000). Another, more limited approach, heavily state-funded in California, is the Family Resource Center, which provides a setting within the school that caters to a variety of social needs and may include adult literacy training (Jackson, LaPoint, Towns, Butty, & Manswell, 2001). Both of these strategies work by trying to bring low-income families into the school.

Research on efforts to create such partnerships indicates that they are not a panacea—and that they are very expensive. An evaluation of the Mott Foundation's 21st Century Learning Communities grants programs suggests that the funded cities focused heavily on the development of projects and were less likely to place a priority on developing parent leadership and community capacity in spite of the positive effect engaged parents have on school climate and parent-staff relationships (Institute for Educational Leadership, 2002), while the implementation issues have led many schools to back off from the substantial required investment in facilities as well as an expanded set of administrative obligations. Still, models of what a "full-service school" could look like are positive and increasingly popular in countries where human service organizations are better coordinated at the municipal level.

Schools as Moral Agencies: Promoting Social Justice

Social justice, an increasingly popular topic in education, blends *caring* as a core educational principle (Noddings, 1992) with a focus on *decreasing gaps* for low-income students (Oakes, Rogers, & Lipton, 2003). As stable communities appear to fragment, schools are the agency that touches most families and individuals at some point in their lives. Contemporary writing emphasizes the role of the school in filling diverse functions such as integrating new immigrants into their new society (Brunn & Delaney-Barmann, 2001; Ramirez, 2003), creating more peaceful, less violent communities (Plucker, 2000), promoting social equity and changing the discourse around race (Zine, 2001), and using the community resources to reinforce moral and civic virtues (Hanzey, 2003).

While this theme is becoming prominent in recent publications, we suspect that it will take up a greater position in the leadership literature as the contradictions of student accountability through testing become more contested. While the public and communities expect students to learn while they are at school, their hopes for schools' impacts are far broader. School leaders cannot define the moral agenda for schools by themselves, but they should be willing to attend to the themes of social justice that are voiced by their communities. When most people think of leadership and leaders that they admire, they look to individuals who provide a voice for moral rather than instrumental visions; Gandhi, Nelson Mandela, and Martin Luther King, Jr., are more prominent than the lists of politicians whose decisions may have had equal impact in shaping our present, but whose articulated dreams were more limited. For the most part, the professions do a poor job of preparing school leaders for this role, although there are clearly individuals in school communities who perform this leadership function.

Getting Started

At an extreme, engaged schools are more than places where parents are involved as partners, or where additional services are provided; they are places where parents and community groups are empowered and can challenge the school to reflect their culture in ways that go beyond the recognition of religion, food, and holidays. These strategies require that schools engage with bridging organizations that work directly with parents and community to foster development. In particular, organizations that represent the interests of community groups may link schools and parents/elders in ways that schools alone are unable to do.

Basic Principles and Strategies

The Coalition for Community Schools is an alliance of national, state, and local agencies in education, human services, government, and philanthropy that advocates for strengthening the ties that once sustained the U.S. concept of the community school. In their recent report to principals, they outline the basic components of a plan for engaging in this work. Their report lays out the actions that principals can take to combine the benchmark behaviors outlined in Table 7.4 and the multiple constituencies that school leaders must work with (Melaville, Berg, & Blank, 2006).

How is this agenda carried out by mere mortals? The leadership implications are largely unexplored in this emerging literature, with the exception of Berg and colleagues, and the unanalyzed case materials

Table 7.4   Keys to Successful Community Engagement

Keys	Actions
1. Know where you're going.	Create a vision of what your school should look like and develop a plan for how to get there. Begin by seeking input from school staff, families, partners, and community residents. Any vision must incorporate the diverse interests of all members.
2. Share leadership.	Invite those partners from the community who share your school's vision to also share resources, expertise, and accountability for targeted objectives.
3. Reach out.	Learn about the community and become a visible presence in it. Listen to what families say they want—not just what others think they need. Respond honestly.
4. Don't ignore the elephant in the room.	Acknowledge and address issues of race and class and define diversity as a strength. Create opportunities for honest conversations about difference.
5. Tell your school's story.	Know how to make your school's vision come alive. Use stories and data to engage all kinds of community groups in conversations about why public education matters and what they can do to help.
6. Stay on course.	Only engage in partnerships that are demonstrably aligned with your school's vision, goals, and objectives. Focus on long-term sustainability.

SOURCE: Adapted from A. Berg, A. Melaville, & M. Blank. (2006). *Community and family engagement: Principals share what works.* Retrieved June 2007 from www.iel.org/pubs/ccs.html, pp. 3–4.

provided by the George Lucas Foundation. However, based on their work and our own, we suggest that the following.

- Developing engaged schools requires school leaders to change how they spend their time. One study suggests that nearly half of all principals spend little or no time in such activities (Goldring & Hausman, 2001).
- Becoming an effective school may reduce some burdens for school leaders. If community networks are in place and others are engaged, this task will be shared more broadly.
- Becoming a real community school requires intensification of leadership, both inside and outside the school.

- Inviting people and agencies to collaborate will generate social capital and civic commitment, but also will increase mutual accountability. Districts must recognize that with increased access to resources comes increased accountability to others—part of the web of influence that was discussed in Chapter 5 and the work that you must do with the district, as discussed in Chapter 6.

CONCLUSION AND SOME PRACTICAL SUGGESTIONS

Most school leaders we talk with want to learn how to work better with parents and community resources. However, as we indicated above, there are few ready-made programs that will work in all schools, and only a few experts who can help you. Furthermore, the basic principles that we outlined in this chapter are very general. Thus, the issue for almost all principals concerns the challenges involved with *getting started* and then *sustaining* the effort over time. As we have stressed throughout this book, the first step is to look for the resources around you so that can build on resources that you already have. Here is a list of ideas to jump-start your efforts.

- *Focus on creating experiences of authentic engagement.* All of the examples provided in this chapter began from the basic assertion that by involving parents and community in the work of the school, it had the potential to benefit of all the parties involved. In none of these cases did the school set out to change or "fix" something that was "broken." Instead they looked out the doors and saw possibility. Sometimes small steps—e.g., inviting ninth-grade parents to an exhibition of their child's work—are the way to start. In others, a wholesale initiative that involves door-to-door work may be required. Authentic engagement of parents and community members, even if it is limited, builds trust.
- *Focus on varied and imaginative forms of two-way communication between home and school.* Our examples show that there is no one best route to success. Instead, our examples demonstrate the multiple ways schools have worked to engage the community to good result. The issue is to keep trying until you find the best fit with your community. Address family skills, enable parents and community members to volunteer, provide learning opportunities at home and in the community, include parents in governance and decision making, and promote collaboration with the community; wherever you think you can best begin the process.
- *Focus on specific community needs.* Gear your activities and plans to the diverse needs of families and their children and to the particular conditions of your school. If your school is at risk of being closed, work to galvanize interest and involvement from people

who might care. Use giant cupcakes for first-grade parents and students, and English language classes (with child care) if you have a new immigrant population. As we have noted elsewhere, all schools are not the same and a one-size-fits-all approach—even within the same district—most likely will not be effective. Learning about what surrounds you can only support your efforts. Get out in the community, walk around, and visit local churches, shops, playgrounds, and parks, and don't rely on prior convictions and beliefs. You may well be surprised at what you find!

- *Make a dream public—share the results you wish to create.* The object of forming lasting supportive relationships with the community is to intensify the leadership and to strengthen the school's culture. The goal is not "public relations" but finding and involving a larger number of people who are willing to dream with you. Make sure that your dream reflects the community's hopes and desires, and not simply the standards imposed by state and federal policy.

- *Focus on strengths.* Seriously assess strengths within the families, the school, and the community, starting with those efforts you believe are most likely to succeed. All communities have a foundation. By finding and capitalizing on that foundation, the work is likely to be better understood and received, and to achieve an early return on investment.

The overall message of this chapter has been focused on developing the ideas that community involvement can and should be part of the school leader's agenda. The choice is which avenue you choose to approach the issue. We have not, through our examples and discussion favored one approach over another. Nor have we offered a recipe for success. Instead, we favor an approach that suggests that, as with all aspects of culture development and enhancement, starting with where you are and hunkering down for the journey is your best choice. In conclusion, focusing on the community as a source of support for the school and a thoughtful approach to community involvement can help you face the increasingly hard work of school leadership and improvement.

WEB RESOURCES, ACTIVITIES, AND REFLECTIONS

Web Resources

1. Check & Connect: http://ici.umn.edu/checkandconnect/

2. George Lucas Foundation: http://www.edutopia.org/; for videos of community-focused schools: http://www.edutopia.org/video?q=video&filter0=**ALL**&filter1=community

3. Joyce Epstein's Center for School, Family, and Community Partnerships for numerous resources: http://www.csos.jhu.edu/P2000/center.htm

Activities

1. Take a virtual walk about your community. Google your local area and list the resources that are available to you and your students.

   Make a list of possible resources for community involvement.

   Make a list of any community leaders that you can find through organizational Web sites or in the newspaper.

2. Take a physical walk about your school community, make appointments, and drop by and visit with members of your external community. Interview them. Questions you might ask include:

   What is the primary mission of your agency?

   What are the major things your organization does?

   How would those intersect with the local school?

   Are there ways in which we might work together?

   Who is a good contact for further discussion?

3. Look at Table 7.4. Address each of the issues, based on what you already know and what you found out in activities 1 and 2.

Reflection

Look back at the Lakeview case (Chapter 4 and earlier in this chapter). What could principal Katie Harms have done to address the community's increasing alienation from the school? Was it too late? What kinds of parent dissatisfaction in your school might lead to parent decisions to move (or move their children to another school if they have the option)?

ANALYZING YOUR SCHOOL

Assessing Your School Community Relationship

Reflect on each item below. Where do the strengths of your school community relationship lie? Where are areas that you could invest some more effort? How might you intensify leadership to include the community?

Our school community relationship helps...		
	Yes	No
Students to become more responsible.		
Teachers understand more about where children come from and what motivates children.		
The curriculum be more relevant for students.		
Teachers and parents work together to help students achieve		
Schools be more accountable to the local community.		
Local community to have input into important decisions within the school.		
Young people be more involved with decisions about their lives.		
Schools and parents come together to plan opportunities for students.		
Young people develop a sense of belonging to the wider community.		
Reduce vandalism and antisocial behavior among young people.		
The local area to be safer and more attractive.		
Adults as well as children to learn.		
Include parents in the education of their children and young people.		
The community to tackle racism and other forms of discrimination.		
Business and human service leaders to improve the chances for young people.		
Schools to prepare new immigrant groups to take part in society.		
Clarify fundamental values related to education.		
Improve discipline and behavior within the school.		
Schools to employ more people who understand the local community.		
Provide the necessary information so that people in the community can help to support the school.		

SOURCE: Adapted from K. Riley & K. S. Louis. (2004). *Exploring new forms of community leadership: Linking schools and communities to improve educational opportunities for young people.* Unpublished report to the National College for School Leadership.

8

Bringing It All Together

Concluding Themes and Thoughts

We decided to write this book because we wanted to help school leaders understand how they can mold their school's culture to effect change and improvement. We have argued that culture change is critical to creating schools that work for students and teachers, and has the capacity to increase learning and achievement. Based on research and the experiences of schools leaders with whom we have worked, we identified two primary factors that have the greatest potential for stimulating culture change: intensifying leadership and stimulating PCOLT (professional community, organizational learning, and trust). In this chapter, we summarize our basic arguments, and show how they are related to the different topics treated in Chapters 2 through 7.

WHAT WE HOPE THAT YOU HAVE LEARNED

As we indicated in Chapter 1, school cultures vary greatly, and those that have strong, healthy cultures perform better than those with weaker and less healthy cultures. Culture, as we emphasized in Chapters 2 and 3, is a complex phenomenon. Understanding it requires that you learn how to look beyond what people say about mission and goals, and begin to look for more subtle indicators that are best revealed by looking at artifacts (visible indicators of what is important). You must also look for the mismatch between stated values and goals, as well as how people spend their time and what they do. Most principals are already attuned to an understanding of culture; they realize that symbols matter and that small behaviors are as important as the big strategic plan. There is, however, more to learn, and we have tried to provide some practical advice about how to take the pulse of your school's culture in order to prepare for cultural improvement. Becoming an accomplished reader of your school's culture and getting prepared for changing your own place in the culture will enable you to be a more effective leader during a period in which demands for continuous improvement are everywhere.

Understanding your school's culture is just a start. Strong, vibrant cultures cannot be mandated, nor can they be sustained without concerted effort on the part of many people. To strengthen school culture, you need to intensify leadership by involving both professionals and students in the work, and by creating new connections outside the school.

Intensified leadership suggests that *broadening meaningful involvement*— through job redesign, distribution of the work, and meaningful involvement in decision making—is necessary for schools to fully attend to the multitude of pressures that they face. Furthermore, intensified leadership suggests that school leaders must *deepen and be more selective* about their own work, thinking through the way in which the larger goals (vision) are meshed with the smaller daily tasks that set the groundwork for leadership *and* management. We argued that intensifying leadership is connected to student learning because it increases your school's capacity to respond to the innumerable pressures that face today's schools. In schools with intensified leadership, more hands are on deck to identify and solve problems. Your ability to access the human resources that you need, both in and outside of the school, are vastly increased. Involving others in the complex work of organizing today's educational settings creates a stronger sense of internal responsibility for the daily work of supporting student learning. It also gives you access to fresh ideas that will encourage more innovation from within, as well as helping you to set strategic priorities among all of the demands that come from outside.

Intensifying leadership will increase the cadre of adults who are engaged in supporting a strong, positive culture in your school. We have also suggested that by developing PCOLT knowledge and skills, leaders are more likely to create lasting cultural change and obtain the student learning results they seek. When you think about how best to focus the energy of your involved participants, research suggests that three key strategic areas for growth are developing professional community, developing a climate that fosters learning among adults as well as students, and creating trusting relationships that bind people together in concerted action.

We have argued that the ability to develop professional community, organizational learning, and trust is foundational for effective leadership and management. Throughout the text we have contended that the knowledge and application of PCOLT skills provide the means with which you can confront problems and make decisions in schools. PCOLT creates the conditions for and fosters attention to learning—across all members of the school community—as the central foci of the school organization's work. In this way, valued ends, outcomes, and goals can be reached.

When PCOLT is present and intensified leadership is active, you will stimulate the development of a nimble school culture. In strong, nimble cultures, members know what is expected of them and the ways in which they personally and professionally contribute to the goals and outcomes of the school. The espoused values of school community members will be visible in the actions they take and the ways in which they interact with each other. The school's culture will be evident to outsiders as well as those who are there every day.

We have included attention to culture, intensified leadership, and PCOLT throughout the book, and Table 8.1 summarizes the specific ways in which each chapter contributes to the overall lessons summarized above. The table demonstrates our belief that these three topics, while distinctive, are also mutually reinforcing and supportive. Practically speaking, you cannot work on any of them without in some way affecting the others. What we have argued is that, given their strong interrelations, it is best for a leader to consider how to capitalize on one to reinforce the outcomes of another. For example, as we saw in the examples of instructional change at Metro High School (Chapter 2), comprehensive reform at Valleyfield (Chapter 3), teacher leadership at Wayland Elementary (Chapter 4), and school district partnerships at Spencer city schools (Chapter 6), attention to issues of student performance unavoidably changed the school's culture and the ways in which leaders acted. Similarly, by engaging in professional networks (Chapter 5) and community involvement strategies (Chapter 7), school leaders expanded those who were considered to be members of the school community and strengthened their available resources to complete pressing work.

The ideas and conclusions presented in Table 8.1 provide a powerful framework for thinking about school improvement. However, sporadic attention to them will have limited results. To create a school culture that is enduring and strong requires that you implement them together and apply them consistently over time. Certainly, there will be periods in which you wonder if you are headed in the right direction. Even harder is maintaining excellence once you have experienced early success. What is required, we believe, is to balance leadership with management, internal and external pressures, stability and change, and intuition with strategic change. We turn now to these emerging themes as a way to expand on the interrelatedness of PCOLT, intensified leadership, and school culture.

Table 8.1 Key Themes by Chapter

	Chapter 2: Principals as Cultural Change Agents	Chapter 3: Diagnosing Your School Culture	Chapter 4: Linking Leadership and School Culture	Chapter 5: Networks, Networking, and Culture Change	Chapter 6: Partnerships with Districts	Chapter 7: Schools and Communities
PCOLT is...	Employed as a primary tool in cultural change efforts.	Strengthened as insights into the school are developed.	Supported by involving others in meaningful improvement efforts.	Necessary to gain access to resources that support your leadership for learning.	The basis for alliance and turning bureaucracy into teamwork.	About alliances that cement the social contract between schools and society.
Intensified leadership is...	The adaptable and flexible practice of leadership *and* management with others.	Stimulated by deeper insights about how members relate, work, and learn.	Enhanced by deepening and being selective about school improvement work.	Supported by your peer's expertise and experience about school improvement.	Inclusive of others within the district who can aid in improvement efforts.	Working with the local community to achieve improvement goals.
School culture is...	Determined by your choices about who to work with and how you work together.	Revealed through inquiry into the nature and meaning of artifacts, values, and beliefs.	Sustained by consistent focus on key goals and involving others in achieving them.	Enhanced by creating external links with others working on similar issues.	Joined at the hip to the district; guiding a school's culture entails effective relationships with the larger organization.	Shaped by external relationships that can support professional practice.

THE ART OF BALANCE

Table 8.1 is a compact summary of our main messages. There is another aspect to the book that is reflected in out use of many examples of real leaders working in real settings. We intended the cases to stimulate reflection on how schools and the people in them handled the process of change. The cases were selected to illustrate the three major themes of culture, intensified leadership, and PCOLT, and Table 8.2 walks you through the different chapters and cases to show how they are related. They are also intended to address another underlying assumption that we introduced in Chapters 1 and 2—that enhancing a school's culture and capacity requires thoughtful consideration of balance.

Table 8.2   Cases by Chapter

	School Culture	Intensified Leadership	PCOLT
Chapter 1: Changing School Culture	• Isolation at Corson Middle School		
Chapter 2: Principals as Cultural Change Agents		• Different leadership approaches (Cook and Wilson) • Uniforms at Valleyfield • SBM at Anders Elementary • Developing a site council at Dane Middle School • Changes at Metro High School	
Chapter 3: Diagnosing Your School Culture	• Comprehensive reform at Valleyfield High School • Personal insight and school change at Hill Elementary		

(Continued)

Table 8.2 (Continued)

	School Culture	Intensified Leadership	PCOLT
Chapter 4: Linking Leadership and School Culture	• Culture and conflict at Red Lake Middle School	• Long-run thinking at Yahoo! And White High School • Teachers' leadership at Wayland Elementary	• Extending trust at Millerswood High School • Lost trust at Lakeview Elementary School • Same message, different delivery in two schools
Chapter 5: Networks, Networking, and Culture Change			• Networks in Sweden and England
Chapter 6: Partnerships with Districts	• District 2 in NYC—four roles for principals Valleyfield High School—partnering for success • Outlaws and rebels—Working in toxicity		• Student learning focus in Spencer schools • Broadening support among school principals in Ridge School District
Chapter 7: Schools and Communities		• Teaming at Lakeside High School • Community and Capitol Elementary School • School site changes in Las Vegas	• Check & Connect—keeping parents in the loop • Including parents at Lakeview

We introduced the idea of balance in two ways. First, in Chapter 1 we noted that changing a culture requires maintaining an equivalent attention to two paired dimensions: an emphasis on stability and on change, and a focus on the internal operations of the school and external demands. Unless you direct attention to all of these, your efforts to change the school's culture will be uncertain. Second, in Chapter 2 we presented the argument that leadership and management have a yin-yang relationship. They are part of the same whole, and although conceptually distinct, are less so in practice. Changing a school's culture requires attending to both. We think that the cases in the book are useful illustrations of real principals involved—more or less successfully—in the art of balance.

When we think of balance, we tend to think of comparisons or contrasts. Does one set of choices appear to be equal to that of another? Does one option present itself as more suited for the situation than another? If I make choice A, will it undermine or support choice B? When balance is achieved, it suggests that equilibrium, harmony, and/or proportion have to be realized. It is a noble and often unattainable goal. Rarely are the choices you make on any given day perfectly balanced; instead, you seek balance over time. It is only when you repeatedly find yourself doing too much of one thing that you (or someone else) will point out that you are out of balance. Maintaining balance is a serious leadership challenge because it often involves making choices between several desirable actions or giving up a pattern that has worked well for you in the past.

Balancing Internal and External Focus

Many of the cases that we presented address (often indirectly) the difficulties of maintaining equal attention to the needs of teachers and students inside the school, as well as external constituencies. We started in Chapter 1 with the failure of Corson Middle School to implement a team-based organization in spite of its preexisting strong professional community. The problem at Corson was not that it was a bad school; rather, it was a school in which both the faculty and the principal failed to pay attention to decades of emerging research and reports suggesting that young adolescents needed a different kind of support system. Because it only looked inward, there were no leaders to help build a bridge between the good features of close department ties to a wider sense of community. Millerswood High School, introduced in Chapter 4, returns to this theme, showing how a principal who was sensitive to both the close ties within departments and the emerging external requirement for interdisciplinary collaboration around improve reading and math scores helped the faculty to make this transition more gradually. Where the principal was active in mediating culture change, the process went smoothly. The case of Valleyfield High School, which appears in Chapters 3 and 6, shows how a new principal changed the school culture quite quickly by spending most of her first two years balancing between demands for change from the district and state and a preexisting culture that was both complacent and resistant to all of the data suggesting that it was a school in trouble.

Accountability is a new pressure for today's principals. Your work needs to address two kinds of accountability—internal and external. The formal external requirements for testing and increasing student achievement are most talked about, but principals know that tests alone cannot provide the levers needed to enhance school performance. Most change in schools comes about because schools and teachers set for themselves and feel rewarded by peers for their effort (Newmann, King, & Rigdon, 1997). Cultures that provide motivation (we're in this together!) and capacity-building (professional development, coaching, and mentoring) pay off. Where internal and external accountability are balanced, change is supported.

For principals, the external pressure for narrow results increases the pressure to focus exclusively on instructional leadership. We have argued that, while important, instructional leadership is an insufficient basis for lasting cultural change because it focuses too narrowly on what individual teachers do with students in classroom. As we have demonstrated across the many cases within this book, lasting and meaningful cultural change engages both internal (Hill Elementary in Chapter 3) and external (Ridge School District in Chapter 6 and Lakeview in Chapter 7) members of the school community in a comprehensive school improvement agenda.

To become an effective boundary spanner who can work proficiently within the school and the community requires you to talk about your school's plans in plain and simple language that can be understood by everyone. It also requires carving out time to meet with community members and groups of teachers. In order to do this, you must share the responsibility for instructional leadership with others.

Balancing Stability and Change

Pundits and politicians have become increasingly vocal about change and the need for educators to respond to shifting global trends lest they doom the economic future of our country. However, educational change is an intricate web, and changing too much, too often, will likely cause as much damage as changing too little, too late. People need a sense of stability, of patterns and routines that allow them to trust the organizations they work in. Too much change and uncertainty destroys the meaning and hope that we attach to today's best efforts, producing a sense of anomie and detachment. Every school also needs change. In the best schools, a continuous improvement orientation is likely to be a core feature of the culture. The challenge is to strike the right balance.

As we argued in Chapter 1, schools are filled with practices and policies that exist simply because "that's the way we've always done it." These vestiges of culture need to be examined and either renewed for good reasons or retired with good cause. People need to understand what has occurred and why it has occurred so that they might make meaning from it. Your leadership is key to diagnosing where the school's culture is consistent with internal and external expectations and with a balanced approach to stability and change. The core of this work is to help people to find significance in what currently exists and what might be in the future.

Many of the cases in this book illustrate school leaders struggling to find the right balance. The case of Red Lake Middle School (Chapter 4) shows what happened when a talented school leader made assumptions about his "can-do" faculty culture and therefore failed to establish meaningful connections between a committee that was planning significant curriculum change and the bulk of the faculty who simply didn't see the need. Chapter 4 also includes the case of Wayland Elementary School, where the principal encouraged the use of newly discovered teacher talents to build a new curriculum focus to an "ordinary" inner-city building. At Wayland, the principal's support of teacher leadership in the development of an arts-infused curriculum allowed the teachers to elaborate the story of culture change as they were living it. Perhaps the most poignant evidence of the impact of leadership on creating balance is the case of Cheryl Lowe in Hill Elementary (Chapter 3). Her personal work in diagnosing the school's culture allowed her to give a voice to unspoken faculty fears that the school was trying to do too many things to be good at any of them. The principal's job in all of these cases was building a bridge between where the school was and where it might go. In each case it was clear that no matter how much teacher leadership already existed in the building, the principal has an important role in telling the story to explain stability and change.

In the best cases, changes are linked to a more meaningful purpose—they help you reinforce what the school stands for, where it is headed, and who you want to become. By focusing on what the school stands for and holding steadily to that—whether you call it vision and mission or goals and objectives—change becomes little more than adjusting the means needed to reach agreed upon goals. Stability to what matters is maintained and changes fit more easily into the school's evolving culture.

Balancing Leadership and Management: Becoming the Yin-Yang

Throughout this book we have argued that school leaders must be engaged with tasks of leadership and management. In Chapter 2 we introduced the yin-yang diagram and suggested that leadership and management were interdependent and complementary roles that good principals simultaneously inhabit. Traditionally, in most organizations, managers were not highly visible people. They worked behind the scenes to make sure that the goals and objectives of the larger organization are realized. Leaders, on the other hand, were considered to be quite visible. As the "face of the organization," leaders rarely had much to do with the day-to-day operations of running the show. As long as we consider leadership and management separate, distinct entities, these descriptions still hold relatively steady.

Our cases frequently show the yin-yang principles in action. The Spencer schools case (Chapter 6) seems to focus primarily on district-initiated leadership. However the district's actions fostered both leadership and management among principals, who became central to articulating the vision of changing instruction within their buildings (leadership), and also became knowledgeable about the details of changing practice that allowed them to more effectively coach their teachers (management). In Chapter 4 we introduced two new middle-school principals, David James and Tim Andersen, both of whom exhibited leadership in developing ambitious and thoughtful improvement initiatives. James's efforts had limited impact because he failed to follow up with good management, while Andersen arranged additional meetings for further discussion and opportunities for teachers to contribute to specific plans. In Andersen's school, progress toward implementation was apparent after a single semester.

These cases illustrate why we consider the two roles less distinctive than many other writers. Consider for a minute the importance of managing the leadership roles of others (the management circle within the leadership side of the yin-yang). We have argued, we hope convincingly, that as school leaders engage others in the important work of the school, their ability to focus the collective energy on what matters increases. However, it is not enough to simply "empower" people to go forth and lead. As the meaningful involvement of others is built up within the school those efforts need to be coordinated in ways that result in their intended outcomes. This coordination task is one of management. By skillfully managing the work of others, leadership goals can be realized and school cultures changed.

You can see that balancing management and leadership requires balancing self and service. A focus on the self suggests that a leader is interested in creating results for the purpose of personal gain or recognition. A service focus suggests a more outward-looking stance. While the most obvious outward focus a leader can adopt is one of vision, outward foci can also include the development, support, and empowering of others. When leaders begin to look outside themselves, to the larger organization for both direction and assistance, leadership across the school is intensified. Service focused leaders strive to:

- inspire creativity and initiative in all members of the organization, built on a fundamental trust in individuals;
- link and leverage pockets of individual activity and expertise by building PCOLT; and
- develop the ability for the school to continuously renew itself.

By focusing your attention on the ways in which management and leadership roles can be adapted to include others in the process, the school's ability to address the pressing demands of educating students well are increased.

Balancing Flexibility/Intuition and "Strategic Planning"

Much has been said about the role of leaders in strategically planning their way to success. Certainly, anyone is more likely to achieve what he or she wants when they know where they are headed. Strategy can be defined as a rational set of sequenced actions aimed achieving the results you seek. Strategy answers the "what are we doing" and "when are we doing it" questions concerning your school. Strategy is the framework for managing the "how" choices that determine the nature and direction of planned activities. The choices guided by strategy relate to the entire range of the school's population of students, areas of need and strength, curricular and instructional resources, and the goals that have been set by the school's members. Perhaps most important, strategies identify critical issues, which are the changes, modifications, and additions to the school's structure and systems, to its capabilities and resources and its internal and external communities.

We adhere to a belief that data analysis and strategic planning are necessary skills for principals (although this book is not about those skills). Experience—both our own and that of principals we have worked with—tells us that it is the rare decision that follows a straightforward path from problem identification through data analysis to an implemented solution. Even studies of business executives suggest that intuition and insight play an important part in creative leadership. Perhaps most important, they are associated with organizational success under conditions of uncertainty (Khatri & Alvin, 2000).

Intuition is formed through a process of rapid cognition that lacks deliberate and evident logic or effort. It is based on rapid and instinctual matching of current conditions to past experiences. It is the basis for the common finding that experts solve problems much more rapidly than novices, because they immediately see and match patterns that previously called for a rational, logical analysis. Call it emotional intelligence, intuition, or instinct, it's the signal inside our gut that tells us it's time to slow down, bend the rules, and change the playbook. Expertise and intuition are particularly critical when no rulebook exists or people are unclear about directions then changes appear unsystematic and haphazard (Weick, 1993).

IMPLICATIONS FOR ACTION AND GROWTH

We have written this book for school leaders across the range of school levels and career stages. Because we believe that schools are more alike than different, they face similar problems and issues, and since leaders often respond to challenge in comparable ways we have avoided targeted, specific advice. As we conclude we will depart from this stance if only for a moment, to offer some direct implications for three groups of school leaders—aspiring principals, new principals, and experienced principals (though we think you should read all three).

Implications for Aspiring Principals

For those readers who are not yet principals, we offer three ways to know: know yourself, know the job, and know what you need to know to do it well.

- *Know yourself.* Examine why you wish to become a principal. What are your motivations and ambitions? Are you someone who wishes to "be in charge," to help others achieve their goals or to discover new possibilities? By becoming clear about your reasons for seeking the position, you can become better able to embark on the work school leadership entails.

- *Know the job.* Examine what being a school leader really means in today's environment. Talk to others about how they spend their days and where they find inspiration and challenge. Begin to set up a support network. Now is the time to begin building a professional network. By using this readiness stage to explore the ways others do this work, you can begin to sort out who has the potential to be of most help to you once you are in the job.

- *Know what you need to know.* Assess your knowledge and skill set objectively. No one starts out knowing how to build cultures that support and sustain learning and growth; they learn it along the way. Join professional organizations, develop alliances with your local university, or join an online community. However you choose to further enhance your own skill set, make it a habit of practice now so that when you enter the position, asking "why" or for help is second nature.

Implications for New Principals (or New to a Setting)

We will assume that if you have passed through the aspiring stage you have assembled a cadre of trusted colleagues and support. If you have not (or are in a new place where your old support system isn't readily accessible), we suggest you start by developing (or enhancing) your professional network. After you've settled in and unpacked your boxes, we suggest that you focus your attentions in these ways:

- *Learn the school.* Spend time in the "wet" stage (see Chapter 3). The most fatal error new principals make is to assume that all schools are alike and that they "know schools." By spending time learning the school (even those within the same district are subtly different), you will find out where your most difficult challenges lie and where your support is located.

- *Learn the district.* Spend time working to understand where your school fits into the larger district picture. Where are the potential landmines located? What are the larger cultural issues? From whom can you garner support? Knowing the landscape in which you live can pay big dividends on down the line.

- *Learn the community.* Schools exist to serve the community that surrounds them. If you are to intensify leadership beyond those inside the school, you must go outside and find those leaders—talk to them directly. By seeking to understand where your resources lie prior to needing them, you can begin to establish trust and support for your efforts.

Implications for Experienced Principals (Working With People You Know Well)

We imagine that if you've read this far into the book, you're the kind of leader who engages in renewal and reflection. However, even the best leaders can be jaded to that which surrounds them. Our suggestions for leaders who have "been there, done that" is to consider the following:

- *Check your working assumptions.* Places change, people grow, and communities evolve. The school that you are leading today probably isn't very much like it was when you accepted the job. Even though you may swear you know the place, spend some time reevaluating what you believe to be true. It may not require a full wet cycle, but we encourage you each year to reassess your school and determine if what you find is in keeping with who you want to be.
- *Borrow knowledge.* Draw on the experiences of your professional networks. Seek help and pose questions and problems, even if (especially if) you think you know the answers. Draw new people into the school's leadership team and challenge how things have always been done in the spirit of finding a better way. Expand, broaden, and increase those in your inner circle and draw them into your school improvement efforts.
- *Mentor a young colleague.* We have made much of the importance of obtaining assistance and support from a professional network. Veteran leaders are in the unique position to be better able to give back into the system. The voice of experience can go a long way in furthering understandings of schools and situations, problems and potentials.

Enhancing a school's culture is a challenging task. In the end we think it is worth it. We argue that the ideas introduced in this book can help you to make your school a happier, healthier place. Happier means that all members of the school community realize they play an important role in the success of the school. Healthier means that all members are engaged in their work, which translates into more learning. Rather than working in isolation, people work together, which means that the school's efforts are expanded rather than duplicated. The result is increased attention to what matters.

ANALYZING YOUR SCHOOL

A PCOLT Planning Guide

Creating school culture change is an ongoing effort. Start your planning here by outlining your strategies, plans, and approaches.

Culture Activity	When will this be accomplished?	Who will be involved?	How will the results, insights, or conclusions be shared?	How will efforts be evaluated?
Identifying internal and external foci				
Considering cultural leadership and management				
School culture inventory				
Getting wet				
Washing: Adding the insights of others				
SWOT analysis				
Force-field analysis				
Appreciative inquiry				
Walkabouts				
PCOLT indicators assessment				
Assessing your leadership challenges				
External resources				
Leadership web				
Diagnosing your district culture				
Assessing school community relationships				

References

Abrahamson, E., & Rosenkopf, L. (1997). Social network effects on the extent of innovation diffusion: A computer simulation. *Organization Science, 8*(3), 289–309.

Argyris, C., & Schön, D. (1974). *Theory in practice: Increasing professional effectiveness*. San Francisco: Jossey-Bass.

Bass, B. (1998). *Transformational leadership: Industrial, military, and educational impact*. Mahwah, NJ: Lawrence Erlbaum.

Bauch, P. (2001). School-community partnerships in rural schools: Renewal and a sense of place. *Peabody Journal of Education, 76*(2), 204–221.

Bauch, P. A., & Goldring, E. B. (1998). Parent-teacher participation in the context of school governance. *Peabody Journal of Education, 73*(1), 15–35.

Beer, M., & Spector, B. (1993). Organizational diagnosis: Its role in organizational learning. *Journal of Counseling and Development, 71*(6), 642–650.

Bennis, W., & Nanus, B. (2003). *Leaders: Strategies for taking charge* (3rd ed.). New York: HarperCollins.

Block, P. (1993). *Stewardship: Choosing service over self-interest*. San Francisco: Berrett-Koehler.

Bolam, R., Stoll, L., & Greenwood, A. (2007). The involvement of support staff in professional learning communities. In L. Stoll & K. S. Louis (Eds.), *Professional learning communities: Divergence, depth, and dilemmas* (pp. 17–29). New York: McGraw-Hill Education.

Borman, G. D., Hewes, G. M., Overman, L. T., & Brown, S. (2003). Comprehensive school reform and achievement: A meta-analysis. *Review of Educational Research, 73*(2), 125–230.

Brain, K., & Reid, I. (2003). Constructing parental involvement in an education action zone: Whose need is it meeting? *Educational Studies, 29*(2), 291–305.

Brunn, M., & Delaney-Barmann, G. (2001). Migrant children and language policies. *Rural Educator, 22*(3), 8–16.

Bryk, A., & Schneider, B. (2002). *Trust in schools: A core resource for improvement*. New York: Russell Sage Foundation.

Bryk, A. S., Sebring, P., Kerbow, D., Rollow, S. G., & Easton, J. (1998). *Charting Chicago school reform: Democratic localism as a lever for change*. Boulder, CO: Westview.

Burke, M. A. (2001). Recruiting and using volunteers in meaningful ways in secondary school. *NASSP Bulletin, 85*(2), 46–52.

Cairns, R. B., & Cairns, B. D. (1994). *Lifelines and risks: Pathways of youth in our time*. Cambridge: Cambridge University Press.

Castells, M. (2000). Toward a sociology of the network society. *Contemporary Sociology, 29*(5), 693–699.

Chavkin, N. F. (2000). Family and community involvement policies: Teachers can lead the way. *Clearing House, 73*(5), 287–290.

Chen, J.-Q., & Dym, W. (2003). Using computer technology to bridge school and community. *Phi Delta Kappan, 85*(3), 232–234.

Clark, S. N., & Clark, D. C. (2002). Collaborative decision making: A promising but underused strategy for middle school improvement. *Middle School Journal, 33*(4), 52–57.

Cohen, M. D., March, J. G., & Olsen, J. P. (1972). A garbage can model of organizational choice. *Administrative Science Quarterly, 17*(1), 1–25.

Collignon, F., Men, M., & Sereri, T. (2001). Finding ways in: Community-based perspectives on southeast Asian family involvement with schools in a New England state. *Journal of Education for Students Placed at Risk, 6*(1–2), 27–44.

Constant, D., Sproull, L., & Kiesler, S. (1996). The kindness of strangers: The usefulness of electronic weak ties for technical advice. *Organization Science 7*(2), 135–199.

Cooley, V. E., & Shen, J. (2003). School accountability and professional job responsibilities: A perspective from secondary principals. *NASSP Bulletin, 87*(634), 10–25.

Cooperider, D., & Srivasta, S. (1997). Appreciative inquiry in organizational life. In W. Pasmore & R. Woodman (Eds.), *Research in organizational change and development* (Vol. 1, pp. 129–169). Greenwich, CT: JAI.

Cooperider, D., & Whitney, D. (2004). *A positive revolution in change: Appreciative inquiry*. Retrieved August 16, 2007, from http://appreciativeinquiry.case.edu/uploads/whatisai.pdf

Corsaro, W. A., Molinari, L., Hadley, K. G., & Sugioka, H. (2003). Keeping and making friends: Italian children's transition from preschool to elementary school. *Social Psychology Quarterly, 66*(3), 272–292.

Deal, T., & Peterson, K. (1991). *The principal's role in shaping school culture*. Washington, DC: U.S. Government Printing Office.

Delany, J., & Wenmoth, D. (2001). Empowering an indigenous rural community: Local teachers for local schools. *Education in Rural Australia, 11*(2), 10–18.

Desimone, L., Finn-Stevenson, M., & Henrich, C. (2000). Whole school reform in a low-income African American community: Effects of the CoZi model on teachers, parents, and students. *Urban Education, 35*(3), 269–323.

Desimone, L., Porter, A., Birman, B., Garet, M., & Yoon, K. (2002). Effects of professional development on teacher's instruction. *Educational Evaluation and Policy Analysis, 24*(2), 81–112.

Desimone, L., Porter, A., & Garet, M. (2002). Effects of professional development on teachers' instruction: Results from a three-year longitudinal study. *Educational Evaluation and Policy Analysis, 24*(2), 81–112.

DiPaola, M., & Tschannen-Moran, M. (2003). The principalship at a crossroads: A study of the conditions and concerns of principals. *NASSP Bulletin, 87*(634), 43–61.

Earl, L., & Katz, S. (2006). *How networked learning communities work*. Victoria, Australia: Centre for Strategic Education.

Earl, L., & Katz, S. (2008). Leadership in networked learning communities: Defining the terrain. *School Leadership and Management, 27*(3), 239–258.

Edgar, E., Patton, J. M., & Day-Vines, N. (2002). Democratic dispositions and cultural competency: Ingredients for school renewal. *Remedial and Special Education, 23*(4), 231–241.

Edutopia (n.d.-a). *Luis Malave on schools as communities.* Oakland, CA: The George Lucas Educational Foundation. Retrieved October 12, 2007, from http://www .edutopia.org/luis-malave-community-schools/

Edutopia. (n.d.-b). *Peggy Bryan on schools as communities.* Oakland, CA: The George Lucas Educational Foundation. Retrieved October 12, 2007, from http:// www.edutopia.org/peggy-bryan-schools-communities/

Elmore, R. (2000). *Building a new structure for school leadership.* Retrieved August 18, 2007, from http://www.ashankerinst.org/Downloads/building.pdf

Elmore, R. (2005). *Knowing the right thing to do: School improvement and performance-based accountability.* Retrieved May 29, 2007, from http://www.nga.org/ Files/pdf/0803KNOWING.PDF

Elmore, R., & Burney, D. (1998). *School variation and systemic instructional improvement in community school district #2, New York.* Retrieved September 3, 2007, from http://www.lrdc.pitt.edu/hplc/publications/school%20variation.pdf

Epstein, J. (1995, May) School/family/community partnerships: Caring for the children we share. *Phi Delta Kappan, 76,* 701–712.

Epstein, J., & Dauber, S. L. (1991). School programs and teacher practices of parent involvement in inner-city elementary and middle schools. *The Elementary School Journal, 94*(1), 29–40.

Epstein, J. L., Sanders, M. G., Simon, B. S., Salinas, K. C., Jansorn, N. R., & Van Voorhis, F. L. (2002). *School, family, and community partnerships: Your handbook for action* (2nd ed.). Thousand Oaks, CA: Corwin Press.

Epstein, J., & Sheldon, S. B. (2002). Present and accounted for: Improving student attendance through family and community involvement. *Journal of Educational Research, 95*(5), 308–318.

Firestone, W. A., & Pennell, J. R. (1997). Designing state-sponsored teacher networks: A comparison of two cases. *American Educational Research Journal, 34*(2), 237–266.

Fullan, M. (2000). The three stories of educational reform. *Phi Delta Kappan, 81*(8), 581–583.

Goldring, E. B., & Hausman, C. (2001). Civic capacity and school principals: The missing links for community development. In R. Crowson & W. Boyd (Eds.), *Community development and school reform* (pp. 191–206). Amsterdam: Elsevier.

Goodwin, R., Cunningham, M., & Childress, R. (2003). The changing role of the secondary principal. *NASSP Bulletin, 87*(634), 26–42.

Gonzalez-DeHass, A. R., & Willems, P. P. (2003). Examining the underutilization of parent involvement in schools. *School Community Journal, 13*(1), 85–99.

Granovetter, M. (1973). The strength of weak ties. *American Journal of Sociology, 6*(6), 1360–1380.

Gray, W. S. (1918). The work of elementary-school principals. *The Elementary School Journal, 19*(1), 24–35.

Gronn, P. (1983). Talk as the work: The accomplishment of school administration. *Administrative Science Quarterly, 28*(1), 1–21.

Gronn, P. (2000). Distributed properties: A new architecture for leadership. *Educational Management Administration and Leadership, 28*(3), 317–338.

Hanzey, D. (2003). The civic mission of schools. *Clearing House, 76*(4), 172–173.

Hargreaves, A., & Dawe, R. (1990). Paths of professional development: Contrived collegiality, collaborative culture, and the case of peer coaching. *Teaching and Teacher Education, 6*(3), 227–241.

Harrison, R., & Stokes, H. (1992). *Diagnosing organizational culture.* San Francisco: Jossey-Bass.

Heller, M. F., & Firestone, W. A. (1995). Who's in charge here? Sources of leadership for change in eight schools. *The Elementary School Journal, 96*(1), 65–86.

Hill, P. (2001). Breaking the hermetic seal. *School Administrator, 58*(3), 40–42.

Hofstede, G. (1991). *Culture and organizations: Software of the mind.* London: McGraw-Hill.

Hofstede, G., Neuijen, B., Ohayv, D., & Sanders, G. (1990). Measuring organizational cultures: A qualitative and quantitative study across twenty cases. *Administrative Science Quarterly, 35*(3), 286–316.

Hord, S., & Sommers, W. (2008). *Leading professional learning communities: Voices from research and practice.* Thousand Oaks, CA: Corwin Press.

Houle, J. C. (2002). Engaging the public in public schools through school choice. *Journal of School Public Relations, 23*(2), 148–158.

Hoy, W. K., & Miskel, C. G. (1996). *Educational administration: Theory, research, and practice* (5th ed.). New York: McGraw-Hill.

Institute for Educational Leadership (IEP). (2002). *Helping young people succeed.* Washington, DC: Author. Retrieved May 14, 2008, from http://www.communityschools.org/helpingyoungpeople.pdf

Jackson, D. (2006). *From PLCs to NLCs.* Paper presented at the International Congress for School Effectiveness and School Improvement, Barcelona, Spain.

Jackson, H., LaPoint, V., Towns, D. P., Butty, J.-A., & Manswell, L. (2001). Creating a family resource center in the context of a talent development high school. *Journal of Negro Education, 70*(1–2), 96–113.

Joyner, E. T., Comer, J. P., & Ben-Avie, M. (Eds.). (2004). *The field guide to Comer schools in action.* Thousand Oaks, CA: Sage.

Khatri, N., & Alvin, H. (2000). The role of intuition in strategic decision-making. *Human Relations, 53*(1), 57–86.

Kossoff, L. L. (n.d.). *Leadership.* Retrieved July 26, 2007, from http://management.about.com/od/leadership/Leadership.htm

Kotter, J. P. (1996). *Leading change.* Boston: Harvard Business School Press.

Kruse, S., & Louis, K. S. (1997). Teacher teaming in middle schools: Dilemmas for a schoolwide community. *Educational Administration Quarterly, 33*(3), 261–289.

Kruse, S., & Louis, K. S. (2007). Building professional community from the top-down: A reflective case study. In L. Stoll & K. S. Louis (Eds.), *Professional learning communities: Divergence, depth and dilemmas* (pp. 106–118). London/New York: Open University Press.

Lareau, A., & Horvat, E. M. (1999). Moments of social inclusion and exclusion: Race, class and cultural capital in family-school relationship. *Sociology of Education, 72*(1), 37–53.

Leistyna, P. (2002). Extending the possibilities of multicultural community partnerships in urban public schools. *Urban Review, 34*(1), 1–23.

Leithwood, K., & Duke, D. L. (1998). Mapping the conceptual terrain of leadership: A critical point of departure for cross-cultural studies. *Peabody Journal of Education, 73*(2), 31–50.

Leithwood, K. D., Jantzi, D., & Steinbach, R. (1998). Leadership and other conditions which foster organizational learning in schools. In K. Leithwood & K. S. Louis (Eds.), *Organizational learning in schools* (pp. 67–92). Lisse, Netherlands: Swets & Zeitlinger.

Leithwood, K., Leonard, L., & Sharratt, L. (1998). Conditions fostering organizational learning in schools. *Educational Administration Quarterly, 34*(2), 243–276.

Leithwood, K., Louis, K. S., Anderson, S., & Wahlstrom, K. (2004). *Review of research: How leadership influences student learning.* New York: Wallace Foundation.

Leonardo, Z. (2003). The agony of school reform: Race, class and the elusive search for social justice. *Educational Researcher, 32*(3), 37–43.

Levitt, B., & March, J. G. (1988). Organizational learning. *Annual Review of Sociology, 14,* 319–340.

Lieberman, A. (2000). Networks as learning communities: Shaping the future of teacher development. *Journal of Teacher Education, 51*(3), 221–227.

Lortie, D. (2002). *Schoolteacher: A sociological study* (2nd ed.). Chicago: University of Chicago Press.

Louis, K. S. (2003). Democratic values, democratic schools: Reflections in an international context. In J. M. L. Moos (Ed.), *Democratic learning: The challenges to school effectiveness* (pp. 74–94). London: Routledge and Kegan Paul.

Louis, K. S., & Freeman, C. (2007). Teacher teaming and high school reform. In K. S. Louis (Ed.), *Organizing for school change* (pp. 175–192). London: Taylor & Francis.

Louis, K. S., & Gordon, M. F. (2006). *Aligning student support with achievement goals: The secondary principal's guide.* Thousand Oaks, CA: Corwin Press.

Louis, K. S., & Kruse, S. D. (1995). *Professionalism and community: Perspectives on reforming urban schools.* Thousand Oaks, CA: Corwin Press.

Louis, K. S., & Miles, M. B. (1990). *Improving the urban high school: What works and why.* New York: Teachers College Press.

Lundberg, C. (2000). Knowing and surfacing an organizational culture: A consultant's guide. In R. Golembiewski (Ed.), *Handbook of organizational consultation* (pp. 701–714). New York: Dekker.

Manz, C. C., & Sims, H. P., Jr. (2001). *The new super leadership: Leading others to lead themselves.* San Francisco: Berrett Koehler.

Mapp, K. L. (2003). Having their say: Parents describe why and how they are engaged in their children's learning. *School Community Journal, 13*(1), 35–64.

March, J. (1988). *Decisions and organizations.* Oxford, UK: Blackwell.

Marks, H. M., & Louis, K. S. (1997). Does teacher empowerment affect the classroom? The implications of teacher empowerment for instructional practice and student academic performance. *Educational Evaluation and Policy Analysis, 19*(3), 245–275.

Marx, E., & Northrop, D. (2000). Partnerships to keep students healthy. *Educational Leadership, 57*(6), 22–24.

Mayrowetz, D., Murphy, J., Louis, K. S., & Smylie, M. (2007). Distributed leadership as work redesign: Retrofitting the job characteristics model. *Educational Policy and Leadership, 6*(1), 69–103.

McGuire, S. (2000). A community school. *Educational Leadership, 57*(6), 18–21.

Melaville, A., Berg, A., & Blank, M. (2006). *Community-based learning: Engaging students for success and citizenship.* New York: Coalition for Community Schools.

MetLife. (2003). *The MetLife survey of the American teacher: An examination of school leadership*. Retrieved June 26, 2007, from http://www.metlife.com/WPSAssets/20781259951075837470V1F2003%20Survey.pdf

Miles, M. B., & Louis, K. S. (1990). Mustering the will and skill for change. *Educational Leadership, 47*(8), 57–61.

Moosa, S., Karabenick, S., & Adams, L. (2001). Teacher perceptions of Arab parent involvement in elementary schools. *School Community Journal, 11*(2), 7–26.

Morris, J. (2002). A "communally bonded" school for African American students, families, and community. *Phi Delta Kappan, 84*(3), 230–234.

Murphy, J. (2002). Reculturing the profession of educational leadership: New blueprints. *Educational Administration Quarterly, 38*(2), 176–191.

Nakagawa, K., Stafford, M., Fisher, T., & Matthews, L. (2002). The "city migrant" dilemma: Building community at high-mobility urban schools. *Urban Education, 37*(1), 96–125.

Newmann, F. M., King, M. B., & Rigdon, M. (1997). Accountability and school performance: Implications from restructuring schools. *Harvard Educational Review, 67*(1), 41–74.

Noddings, N. (1992). *The challenge to care in schools*. New York: Teachers College Press.

Oakes, J., Rogers, J., & Lipton, M. (2003). *Learning power: Organizing for education and justice*. New York: Teachers College Press.

Pettigrew, A. (1990). Conclusion: Organizational climate and culture: Two constructs in search of a role. In B. Schneider (Ed.), *Organizational climate and culture* (pp. 413–434). San Francisco: Jossey-Bass.

Plucker, J. (2000). Positive approaches to preventing school violence: Peace building in schools and communities. *NASSP Bulletin, 84*(614), 1–4.

Powell, W. W., Koput, K. W., & Smith-Doerr, L. (1996). Interorganizational collaboration and the locus of innovation: Networks of learning in biotechnology. *Administrative Science Quarterly, 41*(1), 116–145.

Quinn, R. (1996). *Deep change: Discovering the leader within you*. San Francisco: Jossey-Bass.

Ramirez, F. (2003). Dismay and disappointment: Parental involvement of Latino immigrant parents. *Urban Review, 35*(2), 93–110.

Riley, K., & Louis, K. S. (2004). *Exploring new forms of community leadership: Linking schools and communities to improve educational opportunities for young people*. Unpublished report to the National College for School Leadership.

Rokeach, M. (1973). *The nature of human values*. New York: Free Press.

Rosenblum, S., Louis, K. S., & Rossmiller, R. (1994). School leadership and teacher quality of work life in restructuring schools. In J. Murphy & P. Hallinger (Eds.), *Reshaping the principalship: Insights from transformational reform efforts* (pp. 110–129). Thousand Oaks, CA: Sage.

Rossmiller, R. (1992). The secondary school principal and teachers' quality of work life. *Educational Management and Administration, 20*(3), 132–146.

Sanders, M. G. (2001). The role of community in comprehensive school, family, and community partnership programs. *Elementary School Journal, 102*(1), 19–34.

Sanders, M. G. (2003). Community involvement in schools: From concept to practice. *Education and Urban Society, 35*(2), 161–180.

Sanders, M. G., & Harvey, A. (2002). Beyond the school walls: A case study of principal leadership for school-community collaboration. *Teachers College Record, 104*(7), 1345–1368.

Sarason, S. (1996). *Revisiting "The culture of the school and the problem of change."* New York: Teachers College Press.

Schein, E. (1993). Legitimating clinical research in the study of organizational culture. *Journal of Counseling and Development, 7*(6), 703–708.

Schein, E. (2004). *Organizational culture and leadership* (3rd ed.). New York: Wiley.

Scherp, H. Å., & Scherp, G.-B. (2007). Lärande och skolutveckling: Ledarskap för demokrati och meningsskapande [Learning and school development: Leadership for democracy and the capacity for organizational learning]. Karlstad, Sweden: Karlstad University Studies.

Schmoker, M. (1999). *Results: The key to continuous school improvement.* Arlington, VA: Association for Supervision and Curriculum Development.

Schneider, E. J., & Hollenczer, L. L. (2006). *The principal's guide to managing communication.* Thousand Oaks, CA: Sage.

Schneider, M., Teske, P., Roch, C., & Marschall, M. (1997). Networks to nowhere: Segregation and stratification in networks of information about schools. *American Journal of Political Science, 41*(4), 1201–1223.

Schratz, M. (2003). From administering to leading a school. *Cambridge Journal of Education, 33*(3), 395–416.

Senge, P. (1990). *The fifth discipline.* New York: Doubleday.

Senge, P. (2002). *The fifth discipline: The art and practice of the learning organization.* New York: Currency Doubleday.

Sergiovanni, T. J. (1998). Leadership as pedagogy, capital development and school effectiveness. *International Journal of Leadership in Education, 1*(1), 37–46.

Shedd, J. B., & Bacharach, S. B. (1990). *Tangled hierarchies: Teachers as professionals and the management of schools.* San Francisco: Jossey-Bass.

Sheldon, S. B. (2003). Linking school-family-community partnerships in urban elementary schools to student achievement on state tests. *Urban Review, 35*(2), 149–165.

Sheldon, S. B., & Epstein, J. (2005). Involvement counts: Family and community partnerships and mathematics achievement. *Journal of Educational Research, 98*(4), 196–206.

Sikkink, D. (1999). The social sources of alienation from public schools. *Social Forces, 78*(1), 51–86.

Simon, H. (1976). *Administrative behavior.* New York: Free Press.

Sinclair, M., Christenson, S., & Thurlow, M. (2005). Promoting secondary school completion of urban secondary school youth with emotional or behavioral disabilities. *Journal of Exceptional Children, 71*(4), 465–482.

Sokoloff, H. (2001). Engaging the public: How school boards can call for community involvement in important decisions. *American School Board Journal, 188*(9), 26–29.

Spillane, J. P., Halverson, R., & Diamond, J. B. (2001). Investigating school leadership practice: A distributed perspective. *Educational Researcher, 30*(3), 23–28.

Stoll, L., & Louis, K. S. (2007). *Professional learning communities: Divergence, depth and dilemmas.* London/New York: Open University Press/McGraw-Hill.

Stone, C. (2001). Civic capacity and urban education. *Urban Affairs Review, 36*(5), 595–619.

Surowiecki, J. (2004). *The wisdom of crowds: Why the many are smarter than the few and how collective wisdom shaped business, economies, societies, and nations.* New York: Doubleday.

Trice, H. M., & Beyer, J. (1984). Studying organizational cultures through rites and ceremonials. *Academy of Management Review, 9*(4), 653–669.

Tschannen-Moran, M. (2004). *Trust matters: Leadership for successful schools.* San Francisco: Jossey-Bass.

Vollmer, J. R. (2001). Community permission: The prerequisite for change. *School Administrator, 58*(7), 28–31.

Wagner, C., & Madsen-Copas, P. (2002, Summer). An audit of the culture starts with two handy tools. *Journal of Staff Development,* 42–53.

Wahlstrom, K., & Louis, K. S. (1993). Adoption revisited: Decision-making and school district policy. In S. Bachrach & R. Ogawa (Eds.), *Advances in research and theories of school management and educational policy* (pp. 61–119). Greenwich, CT: JAI.

Waller, W. (Ed.). (1932). *The sociology of teaching.* New York: Wiley.

Wallin, D. (2003). Student leadership and democratic schools: A case study. *NASSP Bulletin, 87*(636), 55–78.

Wall Street Journal. (2006, November 18). Yahoo memo: The peanut butter manifesto. Available from http://www.wsj.com/

Weick, K. E. (1993). The collapse of sensemaking in organizations: The Mann Gulch disaster. *Administrative Science Quarterly, 38,* 628–652.

Wenger, E. (1998). *Communities of practice: Learning, meaning, and identity.* New York: Cambridge University Press.

Westley, F., & Mintzberg, H. (1989, Summer). Visionary leadership and strategic management. *Strategic Management Journal, 10,* 17–32.

Whitaker, T., & Turner, E. (2000). What is your priority? *NASSP Bulletin, 84*(617), 16–21.

Wieland, R. L. (2001). Place attachment and place disruption: The perceptions of selected adults and high school students on a rural school district reorganization. *Rural Educator, 22*(3), 24–28.

Wilson, S. M., & Berne, J. (1999). Teacher learning and the acquisition of professional knowledge: An examination of research on contemporary professional development. *Review of Research in Education, 24,* 173–209.

Wilson, S. M., Iverson, R., & Chrastil, J. (2001). School reform that integrates public education and democratic principles. *Equity and Excellence in Education, 34*(1), 64–70.

Yukl, G. (2002). *Leadership in organizations* (5th ed.). Upper Saddle River, NJ: Prentice Hall.

Zine, J. (2001). Negotiating equity: They dynamics of minority community engagement in constructing inclusive educational policy. *Cambridge Journal of Education, 31*(2), 239–269.

Zwicky, C. N. (2008). *Pushed or pulled? Between school mobility among experienced teachers.* Unpublished doctoral thesis, University of Minnesota, Minneapolis.

Index

CORWIN PRESS

The Corwin Press logo—a raven striding across an open book—represents the union of courage and learning. Corwin Press is committed to improving education for all learners by publishing books and other professional development resources for those serving the field of PreK–12 education. By providing practical, hands-on materials, Corwin Press continues to carry out the promise of its motto: **"Helping Educators Do Their Work Better."**

AASA, founded in 1865, is the professional organization for over 13,000 educational leaders across America and in many other countries. AASA's mission is to support and develop effective school system leaders who are dedicated to the highest quality public education for all children.